Empire in Africa

This series of publications on Africa, Latin America, Southeast Asia, and Global and Comparative Studies is designed to present significant research, translation, and opinion to area specialists and to a wide community of persons interested in world affairs. The editor seeks manuscripts of quality on any subject and can usually make a decision regarding publication within three months of receipt of the original work. Production methods generally permit a work to appear within one year of acceptance. The editor works closely with authors to produce a high-quality book. The series appears in a paperback format and is distributed worldwide. For more information, contact the executive editor at Ohio University Press, 19 Circle Drive, The Ridges, Athens, Ohio 45701.

Executive editor: Gillian Berchowitz
AREA CONSULTANTS
Africa: Diane M. Ciekawy
Latin America: Thomas Walker
Southeast Asia: William H. Frederick
Global and Comparative Studies: Ann R. Tickamyer

The Ohio University Research in International Studies series is published for the Center for International Studies by Ohio University Press. The views expressed in individual volumes are those of the authors and should not be considered to represent the policies or beliefs of the Center for International Studies, Ohio University Press, or Ohio University.

Empire in Africa

ANGOLA AND
ITS NEIGHBORS

David Birmingham

Ohio University Research in International Studies
Africa Series No. 84
Ohio University Press
Athens

Library of Congress Cataloging-in-Publication Data

Birmingham, David.
  Empire in Africa : Angola and its neighbors / David Birmingham.
    p. cm. — (Ohio University research in international studies. Africa series ;
  no. 84)
  Includes bibliographical references and index.
  ISBN 0-89680-248-5 (pbk. : alk. paper)
  1. Angola—History. 2. Portugal—Colonies—Africa—History. I. Title. II.
Series: Research in international studies. Africa series ; no. 84.

DT1325.B55 2006
325'.340967—dc22

                                                    2005032141

Contents

Preface

Angola's imperial age spanned five centuries, from 1500 to 2000. In some respects the experience resembled Hispanic colonization in America, with battalions of conquistadores and cohorts of mission friars and pastors bringing European customs and beliefs to Angola's peoples. In other respects, as outlined in the eleven essays presented here, Angola's experience was closer to that of its African neighbors. The Portuguese influence spreading out from the cities of Luanda and Benguela paralleled the Dutch influence in the south, where settlers created urban enclaves that rippled out into the countryside, coopting local herdsmen, craftsmen, and concubines. Two centuries later, Portuguese colonial practice came to resemble the practices of French and Belgian neighbors in the north as financiers were given a free hand in carving out giant land concessions complete with untrammeled rights over the resident populations of potential conscript workers. On the eastern shore of Africa, imperial experiences in Mozambique linked the Portuguese closely to the British as the railway age opened up an era of mine prospecting, which saw ambitious foreigners and teams of migrant navvies flock to Angola.

Among the themes of modern imperial colonization, one of the most influential and lasting was the impact of Christianity on societies that—unlike some of those in northern, western, and eastern Africa—had little or no previous experience of external world religions. In this book, reference will be found not only to the way empire-builders used the Catholicism of the Portuguese colonizers of Angola and of their Belgian neighbors in Congo, but also to the role of American Methodists, British Brethren, and Swiss Presbyterians in creating empires. Each of these evangelizing traditions inspired and educated some of the African men and women who inherited the colonial territories from the imperial conquerors and carried forward the religious legacy of empire.

A second overarching theme of empire was the introduction of currency transactions, including coins and banknotes, into a broad range of economic activity that had previously been governed by barter exchanges measured in assortments of trade goods. The changes affected not only the old long-distance marketing of salt and iron, but also the new commerce in coffee and sugar, in rubber and ivory, that linked Central Africa to Europe and America and became the economic grounding of empire. The exchange principles affecting commodities were, however, slow to affect the African labor market. In Angola and the neighboring territories, labor recruitment took forms of compulsion, coercion, and conscription that were distressingly similar to the practices utilized by precolonial slave traders. Violence as a means of driving men and women to work ceaselessly for foreigners continued to be prevalent throughout most of the colonial period.

Military might was another means by which empires in Africa were created. During the last years of the nineteenth century and the first decades of the twentieth, columns of white imperial soldiers and black colonial conscripts imposed foreign rule. The legacy of warfare was particularly lasting in the Central African empires, and it was soldiers who captured the nationalist agenda in the 1960s. Thereafter, for a full generation, their officers profited from neocolonial extractive economies. Even where the departing empire builders had created integrated economies, with urban consumers supplied by local industries, the new postimperial rulers tended to revert to the old colonial practice of raw extractive plunder. They concentrated their attention on diamond washing, copper mining, and petroleum drilling.

Empire in Angola and in the neighboring territories was essentially the creation of men—entrepreneurs, engineers, colonels, and merchants. A few colonial settlers sent home for white brides, and pioneering preachers were often wedded to an ascetic life-style. Most other imperial immigrants adopted a predatory mas-culine attitude to the ill-defended female half of the conquered population. In Angola, white migrants fathered mixed-race chil-dren whose ambiguous identities were akin to those of the "col-oured" population of South Africa and the "mestizo" population of South America, and Afro-Europeans in the Central African territories experienced the same contradictory mix of racial dis-advantages and racial privileges experienced by the Anglo-Indian population of the British Empire in Asia.

The most potent legacy of empire—to use the term in its loos-est sense—was the oil revolution of 1973. In Angola, much as in Nigeria and other Atlantic-basin territories, this revolution made the country's soldier-politicians the dependent clients of the Texan oil giants. The corrupting lure of petroleum made an equitable and democratic future hard to grasp when independence arrived in 1975. Warfare, both civil and intrusive, was the first bitter harvest of the imperial age. In the longer term, however, the new wealth may hold out a promise of hope for Angola's vibrant people. Ingenuity and energy have enabled some of each rising generation to survive during Angola's hundred years of foreign plunder and thirty years of civil conflict. With better education, better sanitation, better statesmanship, better friends, Angola's people have rich potential in an impoverished land.

1

The Idea of Empire

This book is mainly about the nineteenth- and twentieth-century impact of empire on the Atlantic fringe of Central Africa, on the peoples whose homes spread across Angola and its neighbors from the Congo forests to the Namibian deserts. To put the story into its wider African context, this introduction, loosely drawn from a presidential address to the African Studies Association of Great Britain, provides a deeper chronological background.

The concept of empire and the associated spread of cultural and economic influence is a very old one. In Africa imperial ideas have flowed and ebbed for more than two thousand years, linking African peoples with their fellows all the way from China in the far east to Brazil in the far west. In some cases the flow has been accompanied by the migration of peoples and in others by the dissemination of religious ideas. Trade has commonly been a vehicle for bringing societies into contact with one another, but in some cases military expeditions have played their role too. Cultural contacts have affected many aspects of people's daily lives, from the adoption of the camel by pastoral peoples in northern Africa to the introduction of the cassava root as one of the main crops of Africa's tropical farmers. Imperial connections have commonly been

1

linked to the search for rare forms of wealth such as gemstones and precious metals. Imperial ideas have deeply affected the ways in which people live, often establishing new concepts of town dwelling or innovative forms of municipal government. Empires have also penetrated the home, creating new patterns of marriage, modifying domestic patterns of architecture, and widening culinary tastes. The footprints of empire have also left behind radical changes of language, innovative concepts of literacy, and new renderings of music.

Two thousand years ago, seafarers from Indonesia were among the earliest and most influential of migrant colonizers to settle the islands and mainlands of Africa. Whether their small vessels, with outriggers and sails, brought them as far as the Atlantic shore is not yet known, but their cultures did reach many tropical parts of the continent over land. Fish trapping and rice growing remained quintessentially east coast activities, but the playing of great wooden xylophones, with resonance chambers made from large calabash gourds, became popular in Angola, and Indonesia's rhythmic tunes invigorated the lives of young and old alike. In the wetter regions of Africa, vegeculture, based on the old African yam, was enhanced by the adoption of a thousand varieties of banana, which enriched carbohydrate dishes and extended the range of Africa's alcoholic beverages. While enjoying their banana beer, forest peoples played board games which had spread across Africa from the Indonesian colonies of Mozambique and Madagascar. On a less cheerful note, this early "empire," like many later ones, spread previously unknown weeds to the farms of Africa and diseases to its farmers.

The Asian dimension of cultural and commercial influence in Africa was varied. The links between India and Africa are illustrated in the wealthy material culture of Axum, an empire that flourished in the Ethiopian highlands in classical times. The lending and borrowing of domestic animals such as humped cattle and cereal crops such as tropical millet enriched both Africa and Asia. The great Persian Empire sent expeditions to Africa from their trading harbors on the shores of the Gulf. It is likely that textiles, the mainstay of many commercial empires, were part of the produce that they shipped down the African coast in exchange for the timbers required by desert architects whose local resources were limited to stone and clay. Cotton planting may have reached Africa by the Persian route, and in later centuries cotton became a key factor affecting the rise and fall of several empires. By the thirteenth century, textiles were reaching Africa from as far away as China and wealthy mine magnates in Zimbabwe, as well as wholesalers on the entrepôt islands of the Tanzanian coast, ate their meals off Chinese porcelain. Chinese mandarins at the imperial court at Nanjing even admired a live giraffe as it disembarked on a quayside several hundred miles up the Yangtze River. Direct trade on the giant Chinese merchant vessels did not last long, however, and in the sixteenth century the Indian Ocean harbors fell into the hands of European colonizers with much smaller ships. Even so, Arab trade between Africa and the Middle East continued to thrive, and on the banks of the Euphrates exotic brides from Ethiopia were greatly admired in the palace gardens of Baghdad.

A more military tradition of empire, quite distinct from that of the Indonesian settlers and Asian traders, developed along the northern coast of Africa with the rise of the Roman Empire. Roman legal traditions relating to citizenship, town governance, slave status, and land tenure were adopted by the Lusitanian peoples of what later became Portugal and were later transferred by Portuguese colonizers to parts of tropical Africa, including Angola. Roman imperial customs had not emerged in the Mediterranean overnight but had grown from deep roots in the earlier imperial civilizations of Egypt, Syria, and Greece. In giving their emperors god-like status, the Romans were following the Egyptians and their worship of the pharaoh. Like Egypt's landed aristocracy, Rome's depended on large cohorts of slaves, and the servile system was later adopted by Portuguese imperialists on both shores of the Atlantic. Phoenician merchants from the harbor towns of Syria created colonies across North Africa, most notably at Carthage, and these later became the southern bastions of Rome's empire. The Greeks not only created colonies in such fertile havens as Cyrenaica but also sent teams of adventurers into the dry Sahara to search for rare trade goods. In the fourth century before the Common Era Alexander's Greek armies conquered Egypt before setting off for Persia and India. Three centuries later one of his successors, the Greek empress Cleopatra, surrendered the fertile valley of the Nile to the Roman legions.

The blending of peoples and of cultures became a distinctive feature of empires in Africa. One fully creolized African from Libya, Septimius Severus, adopted the Roman style of living and rose through the ranks of military and political service to become the god-emperor of all that Rome had conquered.

In the Arab empire, which erupted into Africa at the end of the first Muslim century thirteen hundred years ago, conquered peoples accommodated themselves to the customs of their rulers and adopted new cultural identities in Creole communities. In a pattern of blending later witnessed in other empires, Arab culture, the Arabic language, the Arabic script, and the Islamic faith were readily accepted by many peoples of the towns. The Arabization of northern Africa went further than the converting of townsmen and the recruiting of local military regiments when rural Bedouin migrations began to have an impact on pastoral communities across the great African plains. Only in the mountains of northern Africa did traditional Berber customs, languages, and religions retain their distinctive traits.

In modern times three empires have had an impact on Africa comparable to that of the great waves of Romanization and Arabization: the sixteenth-century Ottoman incorporation of northern Africa into the Turkish empire; the seventeenth-century creation of a Dutch empire that linked southern Africa to the spice colonies of India and Indonesia; and the creation by the Portuguese of an empire on the western and eastern seashores. All three imperial powers, after staking claims to urban footholds along the coast, were eager to gain access to the deep interior of Africa. Portuguese investors penetrated the inland commercial empires of West Africa, sending embassies to the court of Mali on the

Niger and capturing a part of gold trade. Turks entered the tropics from Cairo bringing firearms and chain mail to the empire of Kanem on Lake Chad. The Dutch frontier was opened up by hunters, and when ivory became one of Africa's most desirable exports, all three empires attempted to increase their hold on the elephant country of Central Africa.

One feature of the early-modern empires that has not attracted adequate attention is the role of the great Jewish diasporas of Europe and the Near East. Jewish accountants, clerics, and merchants apparently played a vital role in the economic well-being of the Ottoman empire, and Jews were well protected by Islamic traditions of tolerance. Beyond the western reach of the Ottomans, the city of Tetuan in Morocco thrived on Jewish professionalism and enterprise. Out in the Atlantic, Dutch imperial dynamism owed much to Jewish initiatives, backed by Jewish capital, which had taken refuge in Amsterdam after being driven out of the Iberian kingdoms by Christian intolerance and persecution. A covert but indispensable feature of the Portuguese empire was nevertheless the surviving economic strength of its Jewish communities. Portuguese colonial governors could not permit Jews to practice their religion openly, but they could not afford to deprive themselves of Jewish commercial and industrial services. The first Portuguese lord-proprietor sent to govern Angola, a grandson of the Atlantic explorer Bartholomeu Dias, was explicitly permitted to take Jewish craftsmen with him and may himself have been descended from Jewish ancestors. Little attempt has been made to assess the Jewish contribution to the multicultural Creole communities of Angola, but it is suspected that in the seventeenth century the Portuguese royal inspector of taxes at Luanda had a Friday night job as the rabbi of a clandestine synagogue. In the nineteenth century the street names in the up-country trade fair of Dondo still hinted at a persistent Jewish folk memory.

This book is not about empires at large but about empire in Central Africa. In addition to Turkish encroachment on the north and Dutch encroachment on the south, the eastern fringes of Central Africa saw migrants from the shores of the Indian Ocean bring their cultural baggage inland and create Creole towns of mixed race and heritage on both the Zambezi and the upper Congo. Swahili-speaking Muslims from Mozambique were trading bolts of cotton textiles in exchange for ropes of copper ingots by the fifteenth century, and their new commercial towns were linked to ancient mines that had been exploited since the eighth century. Trading was linked into networks that specialized in the local production and distribution of salt and of dried fish. In the nineteenth century another wave of colonization spread inland from Zanzibar with the Swahili search for ivory. The traders and their local agents built towns with shady boulevards where status-conscious Creoles flourished and Swahili became the language of trade and political command. The Creole towns of the upper Congo, like the older Zambezi towns, were in regular contact with great caravans of Portuguese Creole merchants that had crossed the continent from Angola. So influential were the Swahili Creole traditions in eastern Congo that when a European empire encroached, driven by Leopold of Saxe-Coburg in Brussels, the language of authority of the multinational white mercenaries was Swahili rather than French or Dutch, and after 1908 it remained in use in the Belgian colonial army.

The Creole societies of other protocolonial communities along the Atlantic seaboard bear interesting comparison to those of Angola. While Angola's closest neighbors were the settlements created in the nineteenth century at Libreville in Gabon and Boma in Congo, the communities on the upper coast of Guinea in West Africa had much deeper and older parallels. French Creoles formed the merchant aristocracy of Saint Louis on the Senegal River and the slave entrepôt on Gorée Island. Portuguese Creoles became the imperial agents of the Bissau rice-growing rivers and the salt islands off Cape Verde. British Creoles were descended from surplus slaves repatriated from eighteenth-century Canada, who had been given an Anglo-Scottish homeland on the Sierra Leone estuary. American Creoles were liberated slaves who called their home Liberia and named their administrative town after the fifth American president, James Monroe. The Creole communities in Angola and in Guinea had recognizably similar features; each blended the cultural customs of visiting merchant sailors from Atlantic Europe with those of their African hosts. Attempts at colonization and cultural hybridization began on Africa's islands, stretching from the Canaries to the tropical offshore island of São Tomé. By 1575 a bridgehead had been established on the shoreline island of Luanda, separated from the mainland by a magnificent palm-fringed bay. From there settlers moved to the mainland and established diplomatic relations with the kingdoms of Kongo and Ndongo. In the seventeenth century these kingdoms would be overrun by conquistadores who established the colony of Angola.

The western frontier of Central Africa, which had been opened in the late fifteenth century by Portuguese pioneers, experienced several distinctive phases of cultural change.[1] The first involved the introduction of Christianity. In the sixteenth century the rising kingdom of Kongo was riven by armed factionalism. One of the smaller, and possibly less legitimate, factions hit on the idea of incorporating the Christian deity, along with a host of angels borrowed from Portugal, into its pantheon. The royal pretender adopted the westernized name of Afonso, and in 1506 he soundly routed his rivals. He established a royal court in which black scribes corresponded with Rome. The process of westernization proceeded apace, and one black prince visited Europe, where the pope accorded him the style of bishop. Under the auspices of a black Christian king, immigrant merchants—many of them "New Christians," whose ancestors had been Portuguese Muslims and Jews—established large African families. The clusters of merchant compounds were thronged with slaves, clients, retainers, children, and concubines. Close commercial relations were maintained with the sugar islands of São Tomé, where the ideological system of tropical slave plantations was perfected. In the sixteenth and seventeenth centuries the plantation system was transferred to the Americas, where it took root first in Brazil, then in the Caribbean, and finally in North America. Creoles from the islands and town dwellers throughout the kingdom thrived on their association with the Kongo court and its provincial aristocracy, but they did so increasingly at the expense of an impoverished rural peasantry. After two generations of exploitation, revolution broke out. The sansculottes from the countryside rose up and swept away the court, the princes, and the Afro-European commercial elite with its urban culture. The king and his entourage cowered on the fevered hippopotamus islands of the Congo estuary.

To restore the old kingdom and to maintain an imperial trading base in Central Africa, the united Hapsburg crown of Spain and Portugal decided to send conquistadores to Africa to recover the trading grounds that had supplied slaves not only to the Portuguese plantations of Brazil but to the Spanish mines of Colombia and Peru. Six hundred Portuguese imperial soldiers arrived in Central Africa in 1568 with matchlocks, flintlocks, and other muzzle-loading firearms and were joined by conquistadores from Spain and the Netherlands. Many military men married into the local society and joined the ranks of the Creole bourgeoisie. Black genes soon overwhelmed white ones, and by 1681 Cadornega, an old soldier from Portugal, bemoaned the fact that in his beloved Angola sons were swarthy, grandsons were dusky, and all else was blackness. This black military class of African Creoles with Portuguese culture survives to the present day. One military commander, scion of a long-since black family of early seventeenth-century Dutch origin, almost succeeded in overthrowing the first independent government of Angola in 1977. Other members of the Creole elite became part of the establishment, the *nomenklatura*, of postimperial Angola.

In the nineteenth century Creole life focused as much on commerce as on military rank. In Luanda a flourishing high society astonished visitors who witnessed the elegant balls held in the governor's palace. Among this elite a sophisticated local capitalism had begun to emerge. Dona Ana Joaquina, the grande dame of Luanda black society, began to set up plantations of her own in Africa and to use slaves in local enterprises rather than sell them abroad to the Americas. In preference to buying Brazilian firewater, she made her own trade rum. She also owned a small trans-

atlantic sailing fleet that enabled her to import her horses from
Uruguay. One sophisticated member of society who moved easily
among Creoles as well as expatriates was the young Swiss adven-
turer Héli Chatelain, whose career features in later chapters of
this book. Chatelain was a watch seller (he came from near the
city of La Chaux-de-Fond, where 380,000 gold watches were
made each year), a schoolteacher, a choirmaster, a compiler of dictionaries, a collector of artifacts for the Smithsonian museum, a
commercial attaché with consular duties, and a campaigner against
the practice of slavery. After years of protesting at the inhuman-
ity of slave hunting, Chatelain left Angola in 1907, fearing that his
enemies might poison his food or set fire to his thatched Christian village. Soon afterwards, Angola's four-hundred-year-old Creole civilization faced a series of rude shocks. The rise of racist
attitudes spuriously associated with Darwin now provided a new
intellectual context for empires. Portugal, after a violent republican revolution, became less tolerant of multiracial fraternization
and began to reject the racial pragmatism of the old Creole tradition. By the 1920s the racism that gripped South Africa was almost
matched by the segregationist behavior of republicans in Angola.

Empires that had become racist and segregationist had ambivalent attitudes toward the great variety of Christian missions
that spread into Central Africa in the late nineteenth century.
The relationship between empire and mission had always been a
fraught one, but the rulers of empire tolerated missionaries in the
hope that they would instill "civilized" European values and in-
culcate in Africans a "loyalty" to the conquerors. Missions were
expected to teach colonial languages, create consumer demands
that would benefit home industries, train clerical workers or artisans, and remove Christian converts from the influence of village
headmen empowered by magic rituals. Missions attempted some
of these tasks, but the consequences were not always as expected
and networks of old-school scholars disseminated new ideas and
ambitions. Communities that had lost their old cohesion and their
respect for village elders regrouped in chapels whose leaders
reflected many varieties of Christian charisma. The roots of the

anticolonial nationalism that brought an end to empire can often be found in religious congregations.

The implosion of empire that transformed Central Africa began in 1960, inadvertently triggered by the prime minister of Great Britain, Harold Macmillan. Having witnessed the failure in Egypt of one last attempt to use old-fashioned gunboats to stem the tide of decolonization, Macmillan became convinced that the days of empire were over and the remnants needed to be tied up in new colonial-type partnerships between the industrial countries of the north and the suppliers of raw material in the south. Now that Egypt was lost, the most important imperial-type territory in Africa was South Africa, which had been self-governing since 1910. Although it was a virtually independent part of the British Empire, Macmillan still took a paternalistic, almost patronizing interest in the country's economic stability. When touring black Africa to acknowledge the reality of the new postcolonial order with speeches about "the wind of change" blowing through Africa, he also called in at Cape Town on February 3, 1960. The image of a wind of change had become such a banal commonplace in West Africa that Macmillan's speechwriter, a normally shrewd former secretary to both Clement Attlee and Winston Churchill, failed to realize that the words would play very differently in South Africa. The speech was designed gently to encourage South Africa to move ideologically into a postcolonial world devoid of prejudice or segregation, a world in which neocolonial market relations would be able to flourish unthreatened by the prospect of rebellion. Sensitive Dutch-speaking nationalists in Cape Town's white parliament heard the speech quite differently, as a threat to their dignity and autonomy, a warning to soften the laws of apartheid or risk dire consequences. People in the black townships of South Africa, however, heard the words almost as a promise that Great Britain, having systematically betrayed black aspirations in South Africa for a hundred years, was now prepared to give a voice to African people. The two interpretations of Macmillan's speech met in headlong confrontation only six weeks after he delivered it. The Pan African Congress, hoping to steal a march on the African National Congress, organized a celebratory demonstration aimed at accelerating the demand for new freedoms and the abolition of pass-law controls. White society panicked at the PAC's audacity and met the crowd at Sharpeville with live police ammunition. Singing and dancing stopped abruptly and five dozen fleeing demonstrators were killed by bullets fired at their backs. Macmillan's agenda for managed change in South Africa was dead. But his speech fueled the stirrings of rebellion in Central Africa, and the chain reaction took only twelve months to reach Angola.

The first Sharpeville-type massacre of the forthcoming Central African revolution occurred in June 1960 in a remote northern community of Mozambique. The people of Mueda, who had not been paid for their hard labor on the colonial plantations, went cap in hand to the district office to ask for their arrears of salary. Portugal's fascist-style empire was not accustomed to such popular protest, and the police pulled out their revolvers to quell the impertinence. How much blood was shed has never been measured, but the initial effect, as in South Africa after Sharpeville, was to silence black protest in Mozambique for several years. In the neighboring colonies of Malawi, Zambia, and Zimbabwe, however, rebelliousness continued to grow, and the London rulers of empire had to acknowledge that their grand experiment in creating an imperial partnership in the British corner of Central Africa between white settlers and black peasants had failed. Black governments came to power in the two northern territories, while white settlers mounted a counterrebellion and held on to power in the south.

A different sequence took place in the Belgian sphere of influence in Congo. The rebellions of July 1960 postdated, rather than predated, the Brussels grant of independence. Belgians expected the transition from conventional colonialism to neocolonialism to be free of any ripples of disturbance. Life, the white settlers believed, would carry on as before. Some black nationalists, however, expected immediately to inherit the earth, complete with motor cars, piped water, smart uniforms, and generous paychecks. Conflicting expectations led to unrest, and within a week of independence Belgium had reinvaded Congo and seized its capital city with armed parachute commandos. Worse was to follow when, with the connivance of Europe's industrial corporations, Belgian investors decided to insulate the rich mining province of Katanga from national disturbances by creating a puppet regime led by collaborating black secessionists. Several years of civil war were to follow.

In Angola the decolonizing process, though similar to the process in the neighboring territories, had distinctive features that made it unexpectedly protracted and violent. The violence began in January 1961 when Angola's peasants began to despair of ever getting paid for the cotton that they had been "growing for the governor." Children, they said, were hungry because their mothers had spent too much time picking cotton and not enough time harvesting maize. The Portuguese imperial response to the protests was even more violent than it had been in Mozambique six months earlier, as a rudimentary air force firebombed recalcitrant Angolan villagers, who fled by the thousands to seek safety in the forests of the newly independent Congo. Two months later, farm conscripts working on Angola's northern coffee estates also tried to obtain payment of overdue wages. They too were harshly treated when gangs of white vigilantes were issued with weapons and encouraged to hunt down "troublemakers." In between the two rural uprisings, violence had also broken out in Luanda in February 1961, when groups of young hotheads attempted to free their nationalist heroes from the local prison. The reaction in the city, connived at by officialdom, was to root out any westernized Africans who might advocate social or economic change to the colonial order. The year 1961 saw the first of the great orgies of bloodshed which were to mar the history of Luanda again in 1977 and also in 1992. Violence became the lasting legacy of empire.

2

Wine, Women, and War

This chapter on the Portuguese and the Dutch in Africa was origi-
nally delivered as an "entertainment" in Portuguese at a summer
school for historians held at the New University in Lisbon in 1999.
The themes of alcohol and miscegenation during the wars of con-
quest are key to the imperial experience in Africa. Exploring them
in the context of Portuguese and Dutch colonialism in southern Af-
rica brings out not only the tragedies that beset African life in the
imperial age, but also the ironies that one encounters when analyz-
ing colonial policies and European attempts at justifying them. The
Portuguese, for instance, tried to limit the alcoholism that so under-
mined work schedules on their plantations by curtailing the colonial
production of rum, but they replaced the rum with large-scale im-
ports of Portuguese wine. Their puritan Dutch neighbors, mean-
while, turned surplus agricultural produce into local gin to sell to
mine workers, though mine owners gradually came to realize that
they would have preferred their black labor to stay sober. Both Dutch
and Portuguese colonial traditions were very largely male affairs,
and when not drowning their sorrows in drink or fighting each
other for the control of wealth, colonial men in both spheres were fa-
thering semiblack families with whom they maintained changing
and ambiguous relations.

In the early 1880s a small band of Dutch-speaking farmers, the Boers, made their way across the Kalahari Desert to settle in the southern highlands of Angola. Over the next fifty years they provided one of the links, and also comparisons, between Portuguese West Africa and British South Africa. The trekkers also created a colonial model for some of the Madeiran, Brazilian, and Portuguese settlers who struggled to scratch a living, agrarian or commercial, from the soils and peoples of south Angola. Transport was one field in which the Boers became important entrepreneurs; they created a network of wagon trails across the plateau and as far as the Zambezi before Portugal's royalist colonizers, financed by foreigners, built railways into the highlands and before Portugal's republican colonizers, driven by the dynamic high commissioner Norton de Matos, built roads for automobiles through the interior. The Boers brought the ox plow to tsetse-free areas of southern Angola and extended the cultivation of wheat and maize. They were also great hunters who followed the dwindling stocks of Angola's elephants into the remote fastnesses of the interior. In Angola, however, one important source of early colonial wealth was derived neither from farming nor from hunting but from the distilling of strong alcohol. Back in the Transvaal, successful Boer farmers turned their maize into gin. In Angola, on the other hand, planters grew sugar cane in the Angolan lowlands and turned it into *aguardente* (rum)—the driving force of colonial penetration.

The Angolan rum trade had deep historic roots. Firewater from Brazil had been an important item in the Atlantic trade in slaves before slave exports were outlawed in 1850. Rum remained a bargaining commodity of a new trade that exported indentured workers from Angola. Rum as a means of purchasing the slave-like men and women for shipment to the cocoa islands of São Tomé had many advantages for the traders and disadvantages for the local society. A more beneficial trade commodity would have been cotton cloth. Textiles were valuable and permanent goods that benefited women and children, whereas alcohol was drunk largely by men. Cloth could be stored and exchanged as part of a commercial system of barter, and it did not create a physical craving or addiction but stimulated market activity as fashions changed. For Portuguese traders, however, opportunities for trading in cloth and clothing were limited by the small, inefficient scale of the textile industry in Lisbon and Oporto. Portugal had to buy many of its bales of cotton prints from England and pay for them by the yard in foreign exchange. Alcohol, by contrast, was readily available at soft currency prices.

In the colonial trade a lucrative alternative to cotton textiles and fortified alcohol was gunpowder. Between January 1909 and September 1912, Angola officially imported nearly two million kilograms of loose gunpowder and sold it at considerable profit to Africans, who owned hundreds of thousands of muzzle-loading guns. In 1906 a child slave could be bought in eastern Angola for a single small keg of gunpowder. The gun trade had its downside, however: as colonial occupation spread across the Angolan plateau, armed black resistance increased. In 1913 Norton de Matos decided—despite howls of dismay from the traders—to ban the sale of gunpowder.[1] With gunpowder banned and cloth expensive, the trade in alcohol became ever more attractive. Chiefs who sold slaves to caravan leaders became so addicted to distilled liquor that they offered ever more slaves for ever less rum. The victims themselves were quietened by tots of rum as they were led away for overseas shipment. At the coast, when the new slaves put their cross—in place of a signature—on an indenture paper that signed away all economic freedom, they did so with less reluctance when in a state of alcoholic exhilaration. The recruiting of indentured workers in Africa came to resemble the historic recruiting of mercenaries for the armies of Europe, where press gangs used alcohol as an inducement to enlist.

In Angola the alcohol trade enriched the traders but impoverished other colonizers. Workers who had a taste for rum did not work as hard as those who were sober. The trade became so ubiquitous, however, that the functioning of the whole colonial economy seemed to depend on the rum connection. As a consumer commodity rum created a thirsty demand but brought political problems as well as having moral, psychological, and physical disadvantages. Rum production in Africa did not suit the fiscal requirements of metropolitan authorities in Portugal. Colonial rum undermined the trade in the Portuguese wines traditionally sold to African consumers, and the rulers of empire therefore attempted ineffectually to limit the distilling of rum on the Angolan sugar estates. In 1911 the newly established Portuguese republic took more energetic measures to ban local liquor. To encourage metropolitan producers to seek colonial markets for their salvation, export duty on Portuguese wines, both common and fortified, was reduced. Angola's imports rose to eight million liters of "native" wine a year—possibly ten times more per capita than even wine-producing France was able to sell to its conquered subjects.

One of the ironically amusing documents on the colonial wine trade concerns the way in which the Portuguese wine lobby presented its sales pitch at a meeting held in 1901 in the prestigious premises of the Lisbon Geographical Society.[2] The wine growers recommended that settlers should drink green wine (*vinho verde*) as a refreshing drink for a hot climate. For the "natives," on the other hand, proclaiming their great patriotism and in the name of the campaign against alcoholism, they advocated the increased consumption of fortified wines. It would be useless, they said, to offer Africans wines with an alcoholic content of only 19 percent; to wean them off rum, fortified wines of at least 23 percent should be offered to them. The directors of the Real Companhia Vinicula rejoiced that, by good fortune, brandy was cheap in Portugal and the company could offer strong wines at reasonable prices to help with the national export drive. Through such an offer they could help to combat the pernicious sale of alcohol distilled by planters in Angola.

The amazing audacity of the wine merchants went even further. They also pleaded for an abolition of government controls on the quality of such wines, and instead of any verification of the wines being sold for African consumption, they wanted an unfettered hand to develop their colonial outlets. The market principle, they argued, would be perfectly effective in limiting the levels of adulteration by profiteers. It would be intolerable to colonial wine merchants if inspectors were permitted to examine export wines or impose standards that might bankrupt Portuguese producers. Equally intolerable would be any check on quality made by the customs officers when the supplies arrived in the colonies. In one final plea for preferential treatment, the alcohol traders demanded that colonial currencies be made fully convertible to facilitate the repatriation of profits.

Twenty years later, Angolan officials were still advocating an increase in Portuguese alcoholic imports in order to reduce alcoholism. The patriotic high commissioner, Norton de Matos, back in Africa for a second term of office, proposed a token duty on fortified Portuguese wine and punitive duties on Scottish whisky and French brandy. Wine imports into Angola continued to grow, reaching 35 million liters per year after the Great Depression and World War II. Imported wine was used not to recruit indentured workers for the plantations of São Tomé, but to pay conscripted black migrants who were sent to work on the coffee estates inside Angola. The Angolan taste for Portuguese wines did not end with the fall of empire—ten years after decolonization, Portugal's famous green wine was still available in the bars of Luanda.

The Dutch colonizers of the Transvaal were conducting a quite different set of political debates on the role of alcohol in colonial society. One method of attracting black workers to the South African mines was to offer them stronger beverages than they were able to brew in the villages. The role of alcohol in South African business increased when colonial rulers and settler republics decided that selling guns and gunpowder was strategically dangerous and threatened their political hold on conquered territories. The labor touts tried to switch from payment in guns to payment in woolen blankets. Although blankets were valued in the cold highlands of the Transvaal, they were not sufficient to attract migrant workers to the mining camps. Alcohol was therefore adopted as an inducement to work in the Transvaal mines and in many other South African enterprises.

There was one major difference between labor recruitment in Angola and in the Transvaal: while plantation workers from

Angola could never escape from São Tomé island and so remained exiles and prisoners for life, Transvaal miners could always walk home, and frequently did so when it was time to bring in the harvest, settle a village dispute, or find a wife. One way of limiting any desire by black workers to leave mine employment was to create an addiction to beverages that were available in the gold rush camps. One such beverage was the potent gin made cheaply from surplus German potatoes and smuggled into the Transvaal via Mozambique as though it were a produce of Portugal. An alternative inducement, appreciated by Boer farmers and Afrikaner politicians, was Transvaal gin, distilled from local maize.

As has been demonstrated by Charles van Onselen in his social and economic studies of the Witwatersrand, the Boers who ruled the Transvaal made significant profits out of the trade in alcohol for the mines.[3] The price offered for "mealies" for the miners' porridge was usually low, and maize could not be stored until prices improved. Maize that was converted into gin, on the other hand, could be safely stored and sold when prices were advantageous. The profits on gin were higher than the profits on cornmeal, and Boer farmers liked to sell their harvest to the Transvaal distilleries. Although the Dutch resented the intrusion by "foreign" industrialists into their agricultural paradise, they did like the new market for alcohol that Johannesburg opened up. At the same time, they perversely resented industrialization when black agricultural labor was siphoned off the farms by mine owners who offered competitive wages and strong drink to former field hands who were willing to go down the gold mines. Distillery profits spoke loudly to the farmers, however, and despite their Calvinist puritanism, Boers sold maize to the gin mills and ignored the moral consequences of creating alcoholic addiction among their black Transvaal brethren.

It was British colonial policy, rather than Calvinist moral philosophy, that challenged the Transvaal distilling industry. Opposition to the supply of gin to black Transvaal mine workers, like opposition to the supply of rum to black Angolan field hands, was based on the negative impact of inebriation on worker productivity.

Angola tried to forbid the sale of rum within three kilometers of a plantation. In the Transvaal cheap gin created such a pattern of inebriation that little mine work could be carried out on a Monday. (A similar hangover day in gin-swilling industrial England was called Saint Monday.) Having used gin to attract migrants to Johannesburg, the mine-owning capitalists, pragmatic Englishmen, soon began to campaign against supplying alcohol to workers at the mines. Their proposal to ban the sale of alcohol to black Transvaal consumers immediately ran into opposition from Afrikaner farmers concerned lest they lose the lucrative market for distillery maize. The irony of Transvaal Puritans campaigning for the continuation of alcohol sales to black workers almost matches the absurdity of Norton de Matos advocating the sale of fortified wines to combat alcoholism in Angola.

Political differences between British mine owners and Afrikaner land owners grew more intense through the 1890s and spread from alcohol policy to other matters of high politics. The Afrikaners wanted to preserve their monopoly on transport by continuing to supply the mines with coal brought in on ox wagons from a railhead on the Transvaal border. Transvaal politicians had been reluctant to cause large-scale unemployment among Boer ox breeders and wagon drivers by allowing the British—or the Portuguese—to build a railway through to Johannesburg. Although the Transvaal farmers were eventually persuaded to accept the extension of the mining industry, and even the building of the railways, they wanted to replace lost revenue with new duties and caused much offense to the British by imposing heavy customs tariffs on dynamite needed to open up the deep-level mines. All these disputes—over ox riding, dynamite duty, and alcohol sales—were used by the British Empire as excuses to launch a war in which they aspired to conquer for themselves the world's largest and richest reef of gold mines. Whatever concessions President Kruger's South African Republic made, still the English demanded more. In 1896 hotheaded imperialists attempted to take over the Transvaal in Jameson's conspicuously unsuccessful coup d'état. Three years later Britain invaded.

Once the British, by means of the longest and most expensive war they had fought since the defeat of Napoleon, had established themselves in Southern Africa, and once they had decided that they were not going to use alcohol as the means of buying, recruiting, or attracting workers for their colonial enterprise, they had to find other ways of obtaining labor. Their normal method, like that of the Portuguese, was to recruit *serviçais*, known in English as "indentured laborers." Labor inside South Africa was relatively scarce and therefore expensive and was needed by white Afrikaner farmers, who, unlike black Transvaal farmers, soon recovered the vote and a political voice in the newly conquered colonial Africa. In order to find mine labor, therefore, the British looked outside South Africa and to the globalized market for labor. The three cheapest sources of labor in 1900 were British India, northern China, and Portuguese Africa. The British recruited labor from all three sources in a pattern of oscillation governed by market forces and political expediency. China was initially their main source of migrants. By 1906, however, the working conditions of Chinese "coolies" in the Transvaal mines so closely resembled the working conditions of old-fashioned plantation slaves that the traffic between China and South Africa caused a moral outcry in Britain. A newly elected Liberal government in London decided to end Chinese migration to Africa and repatriated the Chinese workers.

Indian labor had a much longer history of service in Africa than Chinese labor. When slave labor was no longer legitimate, Indians had been used to expand South Africa's sugar plantations. Indian navvies, who were cheaper than African workers, were used extensively to lay railway lines in Africa. Unlike Africans, Indians were unlikely to escape from building sites, since they could not expect to be welcomed as refugees in African villages. The contracting of indentured serviçais from India prompted complaints both from the colonial government in British India and from the Indian middle class. One of India's most famous lawyers, Mohandas Gandhi, went to South Africa to lobby against the exploitation of, and discrimination against, Indian labor. His campaigning coincided with the rise of a new labor policy as the British Empire turned to its third source of ultracheap labor, Portuguese Africa.

The most dynamic branch of the Portuguese trade in African indentured servants, still flourishing four centuries after its origin in the 1480s, was the one that took serviçais from Angola to São Tomé. On the island the so-called servants grew cocoa, which was sold primarily to English chocolate manufacturers. The Portuguese planters had tried to use both Chinese and Indian indentured workers but had had little success. Indentured workers from Angola—sometimes purchased with alcohol—were much cheaper. A domestic slave in Africa could be bought for as little as two small kegs of rum, and by a legal fiction could then become an indentured serviçal available for export. Shipping costs were also much lower for indentured servants bought in Angola than for contract workers shipped from India or China. Angolan serviçais only had to be fed and watered for a few days while manacled to the decks of the boats to prevent their being swept overboard in rough weather. On arrival the conditions under which cocoa workers labored were little better than those endured by the Chinese in the Transvaal mines, and by 1906 agitation against the São Tomé slave trade was growing in parallel with agitation against the Chinese coolie trade. To add to the colonial ferment, humanitarian lobbies were publicizing severe atrocities being committed by the agents of King Leopold in the interior of the Congo.

Britain was reluctant to take the lead in creating a moral agenda in colonial policy. The Swiss-born missionary Héli Chatelain pointed out that it would have been difficult for the British consul in Angola to complain openly about the Portuguese export of serviçais when Britain itself was importing Indian serviçais to built a railway from Benguela to the Congo copper mines. British firms that bought São Tomé cocoa could not, however, close their eyes to the horrors of the trade in kidnapped workers. Many of these had been brought out of the Congo wearing heavy wooden shackles and sold to the Benguela "slave" dealers for little more than ten pounds each. The British manufacturer William Cadbury visited both São Tomé and Benguela in person before accepting that the trade was so inhuman that he should recommend to the chocolate industry at large that an alternative source of cocoa be sought.[4] The mortality rate among São Tomé serviçais—mostly young workers who should have been at the peak of their health—was particularly horrendous, and despite the health care offered on the best plantations, one person in ten died each year. The first year of service, while the imported workers grew accustomed to the lowland tropical climate, the new disease environment, and the bare diet of cassava flour, took a particularly heavy toll. The factor that ultimately sealed the fate of the plantation system, however, was not disease but the failure to repatriate contracted migrants. Recruits were never given the opportunity to return to the land of their birth, or even the land of their purchase. To all intents and purposes they were slaves whose term of service would never come to an end.

One of the ways in which the trade in contract labor to São Tomé differed from other patterns of indentured labor movement in southern Africa was in the proportion of women workers sold by the Angolan caravaneers. The attraction of women workers was that they were cheaper to buy and that they received a smaller monthly allowance than men—less than one thousand *reis* (five English shillings) per month, which was sometimes withheld as punishment for alleged insubordination. Women were not normally hired for mining or railway building but were regularly used on agricultural plantations as in the days of the old slave trade, when one-third of the victims were women. In Angola it was not only exporters of farm labor who bought women. Boers, who lived in married family units with Dutch wives, bought or captured female slaves to do domestic work. Some of the women who accompanied the Boer wagons were Khoisan (Bushmen) women who had been captured during the crossing of the Kalahari Desert or seized from the desert nomads of southwestern Angola. Other servants were bought from caravans coming out of Congo on their way down to Benguela.

The fact that colonization was a largely male affair had widespread and lasting consequences, especially in Portuguese Angola and at the Dutch Cape. Soldiers, traders, bureaucrats, and technicians, who did not take their wives to Africa, recruited substitute women among their defeated opponents. A population of mixed race—and mixed culture—developed in both the Portuguese and the Dutch settlements. This creolized population had very ambiguous class affiliations within the complex structure of colonial society. In South Africa the so-called coloured population was gradually marginalized and finally excluded from mainstream society and politics, although its members spoke Dutch as their only language and belonged to the Calvinist Church, albeit a segregated branch of that church. In Angola the *assimilado* Creoles of mixed race were not systematically excluded from colonial society. They often spoke Portuguese in preference to Kimbundu or Umbundu, and many belonged to the Catholic Church. Their status rose and fell throughout the twentieth century. In that century the Cape coloured Creoles gradually evolved into a separate, racially defined community that regularly received dark-skinned Afrikaners who had been excluded from white society and lost light-skinned coloureds who managed to pass for white.

In Angola colonial society continued to absorb conquered women into at least the fringes of settler society long after that had ceased to be possible in South Africa. South Africa passed a series of increasingly severe "morality laws" to try to prevent interracial association and inhibit the growth of any new generation of mixed-race population. Angola's assimilado population, both old and new, black and *mestiço*, underwent more fluctuating fortunes. The republic of 1910 had brought in a period of harsh repression for the nonwhite peoples of the colony, even those who had previously had high status. Old assimilados were driven from their semiprivileged positions in government by office seekers from Portugal who wanted salaried jobs, to which they thought their white skin entitled them. The republic's great dictatorial governor, Norton de Matos, was keen to enhance white prestige in Angola and strongly discouraged matrimonial mixing. He demanded that any representative of the state in a district office take a white wife and drive out the hitherto accepted concubines and their mestiço children. Racial theory, however, was quite impractical in Angola. The republican carpetbaggers soon fathered a new generation of mixed-race Angolans who aspired to at least some of the privileges their white procreators had enjoyed. The fall of the Portuguese republic in 1926 and the creation of the new monetarist colonial order by the accountant-dictator António Salazar did little to change the social order. Angola remained a society in which black men were compulsorily condemned to work for the state (or sometimes for private but favored colonial enterprises) while black women were liable to be condemned to sexual slavery.

In the 1930s both Portugal and South Africa became mesmerized by the racial theories of Nazi Germany. Nazi ideology was particularly critical of any mixed racial ancestry and exalted an idealized, mythical set of "pure" racial characteristics described as "Nordic." This ideology suited South Africa well. The descendants of ten generations of Dutch men who had fathered their children with Khoi women or Asian slaves were driven lower down the social scale when an Afrikaner "master race" led by General Hertzog replaced the pragmatic British overrule espoused by General Smuts. In Portugal the appeal of German fascism had as much to do with the dictatorial ordering of society and the crushing of democratic debate as with the ideology of racial domination. In a climate of authoritarian colonial exploitation, no easing of racial inequalities occurred and black people remained the workers, white people remained the managers, and mestiço people struggled to retain what privileges they could. The Nazi ideologies of racial purity did little to protect the women of Angola from sexual depredations. When fascism fell out of favor in 1945, Salazar's spin doctors pretended that interracial breeding proved that the Portuguese had never been racists in the Nazi or Afrikaner mold. The argument was far from convincing, however, and it was disdain for black skins that made Angola's women such ready targets for male exploitation or abuse. White women, by contrast, were protected by strong conventions of chastity.

In his memoirs General Delgado, who led the opposition to the Salazarian dictatorship, succeeding General Norton de Matos,

until the secret police murdered him in 1958, reported on his increasing awareness of the racial arrogance of the colonial system
and its cruelly casual attitude towards women.[5] He witnessed the
activities of a commission that toured Angola to investigate conditions in the empire and report back to the great dictator. During the commission's regal progress around the colony, one local
officer was so fearful that his distinguished guests might catch
some "social disease" that he conscripted young girls from the
novitiate of a nearby Catholic convent to serve as "hostesses,"
trusting that their virginal cleanliness would have been ensured
by the supervision of the nuns. When Delgado expressed his profound horror at the racist denial of elementary human dignity
and at the concept of a state-sponsored rape of the most pious of
imperial pupils, he was told in surprised tones that no one in Angola would be in the least concerned if a mere "nigger girl" became pregnant, even if she were a trainee nun. Tragically for the
country, such predatory attitudes proved highly contagious, and
over the next half century most of the armies that sprang up in
Angola tolerated a greater or lesser level of sexual violence against
black women. Only when the new epidemics of sexually transmitted disease made fornication a threat to the immune systems of
men, rather than merely an assault on the piety and dignity of
women, did some armies begin to take action to protect their men.

The effect of colonization on the women of Mozambique was
even more severe than on the women of Angola. Mozambique,
especially southern Mozambique, had become the chief source of
migrant labor for the mining towns of industrial South Africa.
Since the mines primarily recruited male workers—60,000 by
1906 and three times as many a generation later—the Portuguese effectively had to run their colonial economy on female
labor. In rural societies women whose men were absent farmed
the village plots, raised the children, and cared for burned-out old
people discarded by the mines. Men who might have stayed on
the farm were liable to be conscripted into compulsory labor service on the chain gang and so preferred to return to the mines. Only
a few rare men were successful enough as entrepreneurs to bring

back money from the mines, buy a plow, and set themselves up as modernizing farmers, protected by wealth and status from the labor razzias of the state.

The removal of men from the Mozambique economy depressed the peasant sector of production and made labor scarce in colonial government service as well as in private enterprise. When men were not available to uproot the weeds and cut the branches along the footpaths used by colonial soldiers patrolling Mozambique, it was women who were forcibly rounded up to do the public works corvée. And when the plantation companies could not find men to plant, harvest, and carry their rice, it was women who were compelled to work on the company farms. Mozambique also developed sugar estates, copra groves, and sisal plantations, and to make these profitable women were taken away from subsistence farming and their domestic responsibilities in single-parent mine-migrant families and compelled to work for the international investors at menial rates of pay. Under the powerful persuasion of French, Belgian, and British capital and the dictatorial force of Portuguese colonialism, Mozambique extracted more labor from its subjected peoples than any other colony in the twentieth century. Women bore much of the brunt.

In South Africa, although the incorporation of women into the system of colonial extraction was perhaps a little slower to tighten its harsh grip, women were nevertheless taken into the wage sector quite early. When the mining industry reopened after the Anglo-Boer War, many black men were still employed in towns as domestic servants. In order to release this supply of male labor for harder forms of service, strategies were adopted to replace male cooks and stewards with female servants. One strategy was to encourage working-class female immigration to South Africa. The white urban proletariat, hitherto cared for by houseboys in boarding houses, would become a settled and married workforce with wives to do their domestic work. White housewives, however, continued to employ steward boys, and a second strategy had to be devised. Reluctance to train girl servants was overcome by a whispering campaign that suggested that white housewives would not be safe in their homes if they hired male black servants. Panic became endemic, black men were diverted into industry, and black women were squeezed out of their village homes to take up the lonely, segregated lives of urban scullery maids. Many had to care for the white children of their employers while their own children were left behind with grandparents on the reservations. In the second half of the twentieth century apartheid conscripted even more of South Africa's black women, both through migration to the towns and through requiring them to feed retired workers sent to live out their days in the rural Bantustans.

Back in Angola, while many men continued to be addicted to alcohol, women carried out much of the work that enabled society to survive the wars of conquest, the era of colonial exploitation, the wars of national liberation and foreign intervention, and the civil wars of the 1990s. While sustaining the subsistence economy, women also bore children, but even at the end of the twentieth century one-quarter of their offspring died before the age of five.

3

Merchants and Missionaries

One of the most enduring legacies of empire, in Africa as in the Americas, has been Christianity. A generation after the colonial governors and their plumed retinues had withdrawn from the tropics, white-robed priests and sober-suited catechists—both expatriate and indigenous—continued to be central figures in African society. In Angola the mission tradition was varied in origin, in style, and in social impact. The colonial state was officially Roman Catholic, but many of the missionaries were Protestant. Without state support Protestant missions had to seek commercial ways of financing their chapels, schools, and health clinics. One dramatic experiment brought forty American evangelists to Luanda in the 1880s in an endeavor to set up a self-financing Christian community. The experiment failed, but the survivors were adopted by a Methodist missionary society and became the Methodist Church of Angola. Some of its scions were the founders of modern nationalism. This chapter, which originally appeared in 1998 in the journal Lusotopie,[1] *has been expanded with additional material presented to a conference held in Berlin in 2003 to celebrate the retirement of Beatrix Heintze, who spent her academic career meticulously exploring the cultural and anthropological records that illuminate Angola's history.*[2]

The assumption is often made that Protestants in the Portuguese world were subversive of the imperial agenda. This assumption is not invariably correct; some foreign missionaries supported the imperial agenda. Conflict and mutual suspicion did sometimes erupt in the early days of formal colonialism, as when the Baptist Missionary Society spilled over from King Leopold's Congo and began proselytizing in Portuguese Congo. So worried was the Portuguese state at the intrusion of foreigners that it lent a gunboat to a pioneering Catholic priest, Father Barroso, in the hope that he might establish the first modern Portuguese mission in northern Angola. During the "scramble for Africa," royal imperialists in Lisbon aspired to preserve a Portuguese national identity in their sphere of influence. They were willing to use Catholic persuasion and propaganda and feared that Protestants would be less patriotic in their loyalty to the empire. (See the discussion in chapter 5 of the role of the Protestant missions in Angola.)

The simple thesis of Catholic support for the imperial cause and Protestant antagonism toward it has two defects. First, the idea that there was perpetual harmony between Catholics and the Portuguese state is not sustained by the evidence; the church was not able to generate patriotic acclaim for the empire in Angola. Gunboat or no gunboat, the Barroso mission to Portuguese Congo was not a great success. Nor indeed was the subsequent progress of the Catholic Church in Portugal itself. In 1910 the church was persecuted almost to the point of being outlawed by Portugal's republican government. First threatened by anticlerical freemasonry, the church was later also held in check by fascist-style nationalism. Foreign Protestants in the colonies were not the primary worry of the Portuguese church. Most Catholic missionaries in Angola came from France, Italy, Spain, or Germany, not from Portugal itself. Not until 1940, sixteen years after the coup d'état that brought "fascist" Catholic soldiers to power in Portugal, did the imperial government agree to a concordat with the Vatican that preserved Lusitanian patriotism while accommodating the demands of the church. Thereafter a secular clergy that came from Portugal to serve in white settler parishes was supportive of the imperial design. The members of the regular monastic clergy who served the black missions did not come from Portugal and were as ambivalent about some Portuguese colonizing activities as any "subversive" Protestant clergyman.

The second problem with the thesis is that the idea of a deep, persistent hostility between Protestants and Portuguese is also flawed. It is certainly not valid for the 1880s, when Portugal's most patriotic heroes began the long process of exploring and conquering Angola. At least some of the foreign missionaries seem to have been positively keen to celebrate the prowess of the explorers and cheer the planting of the flag. But the cooperation between Portuguese and Protestants goes back further. Although the seventeenth-century Dutch who settled in Angola and fathered great families, such as the Van Dunems, were Roman Catholics, many of the Dutch merchants and seamen of the time were Calvinists. Yet they too were so integrated into the colonial fabric that some Capuchin priests who converted Angolans to Catholicism traveled to and from Rome via Amsterdam using Calvinist ships. In the nineteenth century cooperation between Portuguese colonizers and Protestants was the norm. The Scottish Presbyterian traveler David Livingstone was a particularly vivid witness to the mutual respect that Portuguese and Protestants showed for one another in Angola. While writing up his diaries, Livingstone enjoyed the comfortable hospitality of a great colonial planter of the Luanda highlands and admired his estates without once mentioning that he was one of Angola's leading dealers in slaves.[3] Pragmatic cohabitation epitomized dealings between whites in protocolonial Angola. It enabled missionaries of the 1880s to use the network of merchant footpaths along which Portuguese colonization spread. Cooperation among missionaries, merchants, and the slowly encroaching colonial state was often close and harmonious.

The connection between missionaries and merchants predates the scramble for Africa by almost one hundred years. Campaigners against the abomination of slavery long believed that the way to end it was to introduce into Africa new forms of wealth, new modes of production, and new types of labor incentive. David Livingstone, whose visit to Luanda occurred in 1854, believed that "legitimate trade" would bring an end to the trade in slaves and open up the continent to new opportunities. Traders were less convinced of the benefits that missionaries might bring to their profit-making ventures. Mary Kingsley, who visited Luanda in 1893 and thought it the most beautiful city in West Africa, was sure, unlike Livingstone, that missionaries and merchants had incompatible objectives.[4] Coastal sea captains had convinced her that mission work only spoiled the activities of merchants. Her polemical writings portray the merchants as the true bearers of civilization before missionaries ruined the natives. In Luanda, however, the evidence did not bear out her thesis. Harmony between missionaries and merchants had been enhanced in 1885 by the activities of a remarkable young Swiss of twenty-six, Héli Chatelain, who was at home in both the mission and the merchant environment. The sea captains who plied up and down the coast were as much his friends as they were Mary Kingsley's.[5]

Nearly all the Protestant missionaries who arrived in Angola during the 1880s found themselves as dependent on the hospitality of merchants as Livingstone had been. The long-distance traders who acted as agents of coastal merchants had created a reliable network of communications reaching across Angola to the Zambezi and Congo basins and to the inland markets of the East African Swahili. The trade routes also spread south into the sphere of influence of Angola's Boer community. These merchant paths enabled Protestants to cover hundreds of miles in relative comfort and safety, all the while enjoying the hospitality of Portugal's commercial pioneers, not the least of them being António da Silva Porto. Protestant missions spread into Angola from the north, east, and south, as well as from the Atlantic coast. In the west the mission to which Héli Chatelain was initially attached started at Luanda Bay before quickly heading for the more fertile and less pestilential highlands.

The Luanda mission was nondenominational, initially supported not by Portuguese traders but by the benevolence of a British trading and planting firm, Newton Carnegie and Co. The mission was extraordinary in its size and eccentric in its ideology. With no mother church in the industrialized north, it expected to survive in the old mendicant tradition. The members, an ill-assorted band of forty beggar-evangelists mainly from America, landed in Angola in 1885. Their leader was an irrepressible American Methodist, Bishop William Taylor, whose dynamic energy, persuasive powers, and dictatorial management style enabled him to establish mission posts along the west coast of Africa in American Liberia, French Equatorial Africa, King Leopold's Congo, and Portuguese Angola. The principle underlying the enterprise, in theory if not always in practice, was that each mission was to be self-sustaining. The missionaries would have to live off the land rather than expect handouts from their home congregations in Europe or the United States.

The advance scout of the Taylor mission, and later its deputy station manager at Luanda, was Héli Chatelain, a Swiss immigrant to America who had survived the vicissitudes of his life by developing a sharp eye for business deals. Chatelain's wry account of Taylor's arrival in Angola sheds light on both the colony and the mission. The American band brought no less than forty tons of provisions to set themselves up before their "self-sustaining" ideology could take root. They naturally feared that they would experience great difficulty in clearing their stock of trade goods through Portuguese customs, and it was young Chatelain's task to overcome any bureaucratic hurdles. He did so by quickly establishing close friendships with anyone of importance in the tiny administrative and business world of Luanda, including customs officers and policemen. He soon discovered that everyone in Luanda was more or less dependent on Newton Carnegie and Co., and Mr. Newton himself became Chatelain's guardian angel. When the much-heralded expedition arrived, it was Mr. Newton who waved his wand over the crates and got them through customs with minimal difficulty.

The merchants of Luanda not only helped the Taylor mission negotiate its way through the colonial bureaucracy. They also facilitated relations between the Protestants and the established Catholic hierarchy. Chatelain's closest ally was a Catholic priest who had lost his preaching license, but in good Swiss style he also managed to establish adequately businesslike relations with the official church. When Chatelain advised the secretary to the Roman Catholic bishop of the impending arrival of nineteen Protestant evangelists together with their wives and children, the news was received with phlegmatic acceptance. The Catholic Church, like everyone else in Luanda, was partially dependent on Newton Carnegie and Co. for its material well-being, and the bishop's office had little option but to express a moderately cordial welcome to an enterprise apparently blessed by Mr. Newton himself. The young Swiss Protestant was offered a glass of the bishop's wine. It was, he said, the best that he had ever tasted. Relations between Catholics and Protestants were not hostile, and both were associated with, and to a degree dependent on, the colonial merchants, including the wine merchants, who were one foundation of Portugal's raison d'être in Africa.

The merchant community in this commercial city soon recognized that the mission expected to live off generosity and credit. The self-sufficient Protestants resembled mendicant friars more than worker-priests. Chatelain himself noted in his copious diaries all the houses where he was able to obtain free lunches and dinners from merchants who enjoyed his cultured company. An expedition of forty expatriates that the Methodist Church in America had refused to endorse or finance was a much greater burden on the host colony than a single, rather charming young Swiss bachelor. The merchants quickly rescinded their welcome, and Newton Carnegie and Co. refused to grant the Taylor mission even enough credit to sustain the Spartan lifestyle of an evangelist. Chatelain himself slept on a bare rented floor until he became so ill and bony that the expedition's doctor felt compelled to lend him his personal camp bed on which to convalesce. Many of the missionary party suffered from acute dysentery, and unable to afford medicine, they claimed stoically that to take medicine was to challenge the will of God and cheat the death that he might have chosen for them. Chatelain came near to death, but his merchant friends secured a bed for him in the Maria Pia hospital and even persuaded the governor-general to waive the hospital bills since Chatelain had no money and lived off charity. The Luanda merchants were unable, however, to raise the price of a steamer passage to Europe for Chatelain when he fell seriously ill.

The concept of an industrial mission of craftsmen and traders who could be independent of foreign subsidies and could build a chain of self-reliant Christian communities across Angola did not work well. The greatest problem was alcohol, which was the basis of so much of Africa's trade, particularly in the Latin colonies. When Bishop Taylor presented his project to the authorities, the governor-general of Angola immediately told him that he would be unable to recruit bearers to carry his stores inland unless he offered to pay them with spirits, the cheapest of which would probably have been illicitly distilled cane "brandy" with a potentially high level of noxious alcohol. Dealing in spirits as a necessary means of survival would probably have offended even Taylor's pragmatic attitude to commerce. Moreover, when Taylor arrived in Angola he decided to announce that all of his followers, with two exceptions, would become Methodists at the stroke of a pen, without the laborious teaching and testing that normally preceded conversion. The exceptions were two Quakers, who were unlikely to have been more accepting than the Methodists of the idea of trading in liquor. The problem anticipated by the governor did not recede, however, and for Portuguese trading stations in the bush self-reliance meant distilling local firewater, the type of raw spirits that had done so much to destroy indigenous culture and society on the North American frontier. As the Methodist stations struggled to survive, accusations arose over reports that the Pungo Andongo mission, near the old royal capital of the Ndongo kingdom, had a whiskey distillery on its premises. The mission store was also alleged to have offended against Victorian morality by introducing games and installing a billiard table.

The evangelists, unable to survive in Luanda, set out to find the fertile country in the hinterland that Livingstone had so lyrically described. The two legitimate activities that kept the self-sufficient mission stations functioning for the next ten years were teaching and gardening. The evangelists offered school lessons to the children of traders, but the children who were enrolled, even in the great market town of Dondo, could usually be counted on the fingers of two hands, and when it was time to pay school fees the children were liable to absent themselves. Gardening therefore became the basis of self-reliance. The evangelists, however, were not robust, their diet was seriously inadequate, their health was often poor, and several of them died or saw their children die. Like other colonists they tried to hire labor to work their plots for them. To attract workers the missions had to offer payment in good American calico. Mission gardens could not escape the merchant nexus or the need for foreign support, and the great experiment failed. Bishop Taylor retired in 1896, the concept of self-reliance was dropped, and the Methodist Church of America formally adopted the Protestant mission stations of the Luanda hinterland. With this foreign sponsorship the mission communities in the Malange district began to flourish, to win converts, and eventually to establish a prestigious high school that trained some members of Angola's modernizing elite.

During his years with the self-reliant mission Héli Chatelain became a great traveler. Despite being very lame from childhood illness, he did much of his traveling on foot and was affectionately known in Angola as "Long-leg and Short-leg." Although he was a quintessentially humane man and remarkably free of the exploitative racial prejudices that were normal in both America and Africa during his lifetime, he did avail himself of a traveling hammock for his long journeys into the Kimbundu-speaking hinterland of Luanda. Hammocks required stout porters, and on his travels through the high forest and tall grass toward Malange he was commonly frustrated at the difficulty in getting his caravan crew underway on cold, dew-laden mornings. Where the country was steep, he did ease the burden on his bearers by undertaking the most trying stretches on foot. Etiquette among fellow travelers, however, was a mystery to him; white men, lounging back on their pillows en route to the coast, scarcely raised a hand to greet the eccentric Swiss when their paths crossed. When Chatelain reached his final destination near Malange, he set about recruiting the services of a cobbler's son, Jeremiah, to be his linguistic informant. Over the next dozen years the two men produced grammars and dictionaries of the Kimbundu language, which were used not only in Christian missions but in the Portuguese colonial administration.

Historically, water transport has usually been easier and cheaper than land transport, and Chatelain, who had grown up among the great Alpine lakes, tried to avail himself of boats where possible. In Africa, however, small-scale shipping along the rivers met with great frustration. The Kwanza River, on the route between Luanda and the port of Dondo, downstream from Malange, had coastal sand bars that were dangerous to negotiate. Once boats did enter the river, the light winds and strong currents made progress slow. Overnight shelters were primitive. Most traders, notably those responsible for exporting coffee, found that head loading their sacks to the coast was safer, faster, and more reliable than river transport. Attempts to use small steam-driven boats on the river also met with poor results, as the ever-ambitious Chatelain discovered on a frustrating, mosquito-plagued trip to visit a slave-worked sugar plantation owned by one of his city friends. The late-Victorian belief in technological modernity was not checked by handicaps on the river, however, and colonial visionaries dreamed of building a steam railway that would run from Luanda into the deep interior beyond Malange. The pretentiously named Royal Transafrica Railway Company was designed to link the magnificent harbor of Luanda with the interior of Congo and even with the east coast of Africa. The scheme, however, was a catastrophic failure. The line was built so cheaply that it could not withstand storms and floods. Financially, it was such a poor risk that investors had to be promised a profitable return by the government whether or not they ran any trains or generated any operating revenue. And economically the line was ill conceived in aiming to tap a coffee zone whose produce had such a high ratio of value to weight that head porterage was a perfectly viable transport option, while bulk freight from the mines remained inaccessible on the far side of the Belgian colonial frontier. Chatelain's one attempt to travel by rail as a passenger was fraught with mishaps.

As transport officer for the so-called Methodist mission, Chatelain became familiar with all the lightermen who ferried cargoes from ships anchored in Luanda bay to the city beaches. Persuading the crews of these small boats to hurry when the great steamers were getting ready to depart was a fine art. The risk of being separated from one's cabin trunks was a frightening prospect for any white person who had reached the farthest ends of western Africa. The boatmen learned how to drive hard bargains to frustrate Chatelain's Swiss prudence in matters of finance. During his service the mission transport manager got to know many of the officers who staffed the steamships that served the coast. When Chatelain was taken seriously ill, a ship's captain took him on board for a rest cruise down the coast to the slightly healthier port of Benguela. The trip widened Chatelain's horizons, and during the second half of his African career he worked on the Benguela plateau rather than in the Luanda hinterland.

While Bishop Taylor and his acolyte Chatelain established worker missions in western Angola, alternative variants of Protestantism took root in eastern Angola. In the fifty years to 1930, the largest Protestant mission in the country was that of the Plymouth Brethren, or Darbyites, or *frères larges*, as they were sometimes called in Europe. The Brethren arrived in Angola along the trails from the south that had once brought Livingstone up from South Africa. Their journeys were facilitated by Silva Porto, the great Portuguese transcontinental merchant, who helped the missionaries organize transport and find hospitality. In the far interior, however, he was unable to find a cobbler when the young English missionary Frederick Arnot's boots wore out. Arnot tried walking barefoot like everyone else on the African trade paths, but the hot sand blistered his feet. Old Silva Porto was in time able to rent him a riding ox that could plod its way through a thousand miles of thorn bush and even swim rivers. Arnot and the Brethren eventually reached the eastern highland of Angola and set up their headquarters close to Silva Porto's trading emporium.[6]

The Plymouth Brethren were perfectly aware that their necessary association with traders involved adopting a muted attitude toward the slave trade. Arnot's friend Silva Porto had been a supplier of slaves to the west coast for half a century. The young missionary persuaded himself, however, that the trade in alcohol had been an even worse evil than the trade in slaves. He even saw glimmers of hope when Silva Porto claimed that he planned to grant freedom to his personal household slaves. The ancient merchant also repeated the old claim that he was rescuing slaves from cannibalism and even converting them to Christianity by putting "holy salt," blessed by a priest, on their tongues. "I, too, am a missionary," said Silva Porto beguilingly. The centuries-old traditions of justifying slavery as Christian redemption and providing wholesale Catholic "baptism" by giving magic salt were still being practiced in the last quarter of the nineteenth century. Neither the old Portuguese nor the young Englishman seemed much concerned about the differences of Christian belief that later caused conflict between Angola's Catholics and Protestants.

Salt was not only a source of religious power but a means of economic survival in the Angolan interior. The Plymouth Brethren tried to use mules, rather than bearers, to ensure that their supplies of trade salt got through to the highland stations from the great West Coast salt pans of Benguela. When one caravan of ten mules failed to complete the journey, the missionaries were compelled to hire human porters as the merchants did. The missionaries' porters were free men to whom they paid the standard rate for carrying a headload up from the coast. This standard rate, however, had become much depressed as the great slave raids of the late nineteenth century swept through the highlands. Men regularly allowed themselves to be conscripted as porters in order to avoid being sold to plantation contractors and exported for the remainder of their natural lives. The porters attempted to bargain with the missionaries for better wages, but even though the Brethren were probably the best endowed of all the Angolan missions, the labor market did not allow much humanitarian generosity.

A pragmatic association with merchants enabled missionaries to survive economically in Angola's deep interior. Merchants sometimes helped missionaries to survive politically as well. In 1890 a newly elected king of Bihé decided that he would expel all aliens from his territory, Portuguese invaders and British missionaries alike. It was Silva Porto, the old settler-merchant, who warned the Brethren of the impending war and enabled them to negotiate a treaty of friendship with the king. While the missionaries stayed on, the Portuguese were driven out and even Silva Porto, who had spent his entire trading life in Bihé, felt that his merchant network was at risk. Rather than leave his highland home, he attempted to blow himself up spectacularly by igniting a few kegs of gunpowder. His friends at the mission made valiant attempts to save his life, but his burns were too severe. The loyalty of the Protestant missionaries to their Portuguese patron did not protect them from the wrath of the colonial invaders when they returned. The Portuguese state sent a whole army up from the coast to recover raiding grounds where slaves were traditionally captured. In November 1890 a thousand colonial foot soldiers and ninety Boer horse commandos arrived in Bihé to wreak revenge against the people who had caused them such grievous losses. The Brethren wisely negotiated with the posse of Boers, offering them excellent meals cooked by a European missionary wife. As tempers cooled, settlers and missionaries were able to orchestrate a peace plan and persuade the king of Bihé to come out of hiding and surrender. Led away by the Portuguese commander of the punitive expedition, the king entrusted his gun to Frederick Arnot, the missionary peacemaker. Arnot, like other missionaries in Angola, did not question the right of the colonial powers to impose their rule over Africa.

Cooperation between merchants and missionaries, and mutual toleration between Portuguese and Protestants, were in evidence even during the spectacular conflict that occurred in the kingdom of Bailundu, next door to the Brethren's host kingdom of Bihé. A mission of American Congregationalists had maintained reasonably good relations with the Methodists, the Swiss, and the Brethren, though the local Catholic Church viewed it with suspicion. When the anti-Portuguese rebellion broke out in 1902, the Protestant missionaries, good, loyal believers in the rights of the colonizing powers, did their best to help restore imperial law and order. They even supplied military intelligence to the commanders of the invading colonial army concerning the movements of the Bailundu regiments. When a besieged Portuguese unit ran short of supplies, the missionaries provided it with food and trade goods from the mission warehouse. Such cooperation, however, was no longer enough to convince the official Portuguese mind that Protestants were anything but subversive foreigners. The era of pragmatic collaboration began to give way to one of suspicion, and relations among missionaries, merchants, and administrators became more brittle than they had been through the nineteenth century. Chatelain nevertheless returned to Africa in 1897 with a new mandate to create a self-sustaining mission in Angola's southern highland.

4

A Swiss Community in Highland Angola

This chapter, which was first published in the proceedings of a conference on African history held in Lisbon in September 1999,[1] explores the last ten years of Héli Chatelain's entrepreneurial endeavors as he tried to sustain his small Christian community on the edge of the southern highlands. Although his village of local peasants and emancipated slaves was isolated and remote, Chatelain was able to maintain a worldwide correspondence in English, French, German, Dutch, and Portuguese with his theological sponsors and commercial suppliers in Switzerland and America. He also understood the people of the local Ovimbundu kingdoms and wrote hymns for them in their own vernaculars. After his death the Swiss churches took over Chatelain's venture, and some of the leading politicians of modern Angola went to school at the Swiss mission before being sent to Switzerland for further training.

The concept of establishing self-sufficient Christian communities in Angola did not die out immediately when Bishop Taylor's Malange mission, which Héli Chatelain had helped to create, was converted into an officially sponsored Methodist field of proselytizing. Ten years after he had visited Benguela as a convalescent, Chatelain returned to Angola's southern harbor city determined to try out for himself the ideals that had inspired the now-retired Bishop Taylor. Resolving the problem of how to maintain a balance between missionary idealism and merchant pragmatism had not become any easier. When Chatelain arrived in Benguela in 1897, the slave trade had revived so vigorously that the city was shipping out some 4,000 men and women each year. The aim of the new mission was to stem the flow of this trade and create a chain of hostels for escaped slaves all the way from Benguela to the great raiding grounds among the Nganguela people of the upper Cunene and Zambezi rivers. Such was the dependence of missionaries on merchants, and of merchants on the sale of slaves, however, that no such chain of safe havens could be established. Without ox trails and bush stores, any mission penetration was virtually impossible. Chatelain's Swiss-American mission only ever set up one station. It was located not in the remote hunting grounds of the slave catchers, but in settler territory on the high plateau, and its best customers were not free Africans, but Boer immigrants from South Africa. The Dutch settler community at Caconda with which the mission traded was an offshoot of a larger Boer colony at Humpata on Angola's southernmost plateau.

The dependence of the Swiss mission on the Boer colony began from the moment when Chatelain landed at Benguela and found that rinderpest fever had decimated Angola's stock of oxen. He had a long wait before he could negotiate the hire of Boer wagons to haul his equipment through the coastal scrub and up the escarpment to Kalukembe, the site near Caconda that he had chosen for his station. Once established, the mission became a trading post that depended on its Boer customers for its economic viability. Had the mission agreed to harbor slave refugees from the Boer slave farms, the commercial side of the enterprise would have lost its most lucrative business clients. Although Boer customers did not like the mission's social ideology, they had little direct access to suppliers in Europe and no network of international credit that would enable them to order goods from abroad. They therefore welcomed Chatelain's business acumen, his ability to make credit deals with overseas suppliers, and his familiarity with the necessary settler crafts. His workshop installed anvils and forges with which Boer carts could be repaired, and his mission artisans kept the transport system of southern Angola running. Chatelain's import-and-export business underpinned the semi-self-sufficient mission's finances. To remain solvent, the mission had to play down any antislaving ideals its sponsoring League of Friends had dreamt of. These sponsors, to the great chagrin of the Portuguese, had even named the station "Lincoln," after the American president who had outlawed slavery in the United States.

Although Chatelain had little success in protecting captive Angolans from slavery, he did develop commercial relations with his free black neighbors. He traveled round the villages with his own ox cart buying beans and maize each season as the crop was harvested. The wares that he peddled in exchange were those that would have been seen at any roadside fair in his native Switzerland. Unlike all other traders, he refused to sell wine and brandy, but his mobile wagon shop carried sugar, salt, cooking oil, dried meat, and soap as basic necessities, as well as ironmongery, padlocks, spades, hoes, wire, traps, penknives, and cutlery. His stock of crockery included cups, plates, casseroles, and bowls. Vanity was catered for with ten different kinds of glass beads, shirt and coat buttons, bracelets, earrings, belts, and colored kerchiefs. Textiles ranged from cotton prints and woolen blankets to shirts, trousers, coats, and caps. The traveling bazaar was complete with supplies of flint, lead, gunpowder, medicines, sewing needles, matchsticks, mirrors, writing paper, and mouth organs.

A perambulating bean merchant with a forty-acre small holding staffed by casual black labor from neighboring villages was no great threat to the Portuguese merchant community. But Chatelain was more than that. He was a missionary with world connections who still aspired to end the Angolan slave trade. In 1903 Chatelain feared that at any time an "accident" might happen to him or to his mission station. He let it be known that should any violence occur, or should his mission be burnt down by the slave raiders, a report that he had lodged with the Swiss consul at

Lisbon would be made public. This report would give full details of the violence affecting local trading conditions and specify the manner in which colonial and military officials in Angola not only tolerated the slave trade but personally benefited from it. Creaming off a share of the slave profits could make an officer's tour of duty in a harsh colony staffed by convicts economically attractive.

In between bartering maize for crockery and corresponding with foreign businessmen about the slave trade, Chatelain developed an almost limitless range of commercial sidelines in his efforts to create a self-sustaining Christian community. Among his papers is a manuscript catalogue of postage stamps issued by the Angolan post office. It describes the different colors, reigns, denominations, embossments, perforations, printing errors, and overprintings found on the stamps in his commercial collection. Each stamp bears a retail price in Swiss francs at which Chatelain would be able to supply specimens to collectors. Stamp collecting seems a far cry from Chatelain's initial crusade to challenge polygamy, witchcraft, alcoholism, and all the running sores that missionary societies had tolerated for too long. His great ambition, however, was to sanctify the practice of commerce as the economic mainstay of mission. This was a much harder challenge than sanctifying the practice of farming, craftwork, teaching, or nursing. Chatelain found it difficult to attract shopkeepers to come from Switzerland and accept his own bachelor asceticism, or to recruit mission workers willing to acknowledge his belief that it was colonization that represented the road to liberty for Africa's people. One had to be patient and pragmatic when waiting for the benefits of "civilization" to trickle down. Chatelain's commercial path on the Angolan highlands proved to be a much stonier one than that of the Swiss missionaries from Basel who created an integrated network of country stores and village chapels on the Gold Coast in modern Ghana.[2]

If transport had been a problem in the Kwanza valley when Chatelain was helping establish the Malange mission, it proved to be an even greater problem on the southern highlands. The coastal rivers tumbled down into the sea, and the inland ones created unpredictable flood plains across which ferry services were jealously guarded by boatmen licensed and taxed by an embryonic colonial state based at the old eighteenth-century trading fortress of Caconda. Rather than use the expensive and somewhat dehumanizing services of hammock bearers, Chatelain traveled around the highlands on a donkey. He presented a bizarre appearance: a short-sighted, bespectacled figure wearing a three-piece suit decorated with a gold watch chain and shod in long, elasticized boots that almost dragged along the ground beneath him. The donkey, however, had its limitations as a pack animal, and in 1881 a revolution in highland transport had occurred. Several dozen extended families of South African Boers had crossed the Namibian "thirstlands" and reached Angola thanks to the novel technology of the ox wagon. Similar wagons were used on the plateau farms of Switzerland, and at least one ambitious expedition had used them to cross the breadth of Europe and settle a Swiss colony on the shores of the Black Sea under the patronage of Tsar Alexander. Wagons, however, had three major requirements: large-scale financial credit for the capital outlay, veterinary knowledge to keep the teams of twenty oxen healthy, and carpenters or blacksmiths to repair the wagon beds and refit the great metal hoops that rimmed the wooden wheels. None of these services could be adequately supplied by African merchants, stockmen, and artisans, nor indeed by Portuguese-speaking settlers moving up from the Benguela coast. Chatelain therefore aspired to create a Christian community in the highland that would be financed by a wagon workshop to serve the late-nineteenth-century transport riders.

Setting up an ox wagon business in early colonial Angola was not easy, and the economics of transport were even more problematic than the fraught relations with slave-owning clients. The steep, ever-shifting, deeply rutted tracks leading up from the coast to the highland were far from ideally suited to establishing a transport system that could rival, let alone replace, the footpaths used by runners and bearers. When his wagons were not in service, Chatelain advised American visitors that they could expect to pay porters three thousand reis per thirty-kilogram head load to bring luggage up to his station from Benguela. This method was often faster and cheaper than bringing goods up by wagon, but porters were hard to recruit and were sometimes less trustworthy than wagons, so travelers and merchants often paid the wagon rate for each ton per league. On a good trip Chatelain could take his wagon down to Benguela from Kalukembe, a hundred miles, in ten days. Returning uphill was likely to take thirty days. The journey was not possible when there was no grass for the oxen to eat along the way or when the holes in the river beds had dried up and the animals were left gasping with thirst. When the rains began, travel was equally difficult. Although some streams had small bridges for porters to walk across, the wagons had to go to the bottom of each ravine to a suitable ford before being hauled up on the other side. It was often necessary to unload the ton-and-a-half of boxes, sacks, and bales of merchandise before each river crossing, lest the vehicle sink so deep into the mud that even extra oxen could not pull it out. Inland from Kalukembe the journey could be equally slow, not so much because of drought or flood as because of the constant need to cut down trees to open a new trail. When Chatelain's Swiss assistant Ali Pieren took the mission wagon from Kalukembe to Bihé in search of business, the journey of 150 miles took him thirty-three days. A column of porters could have done it in half the time, but a wagon with a full payload could carry as much as fifty men could carry on foot.

One key to the wagon trade was the quality of the wagons. Before the advent of the motor car, one of the most prestigious manufacturers of carriages and wagons in the United States was the firm of Studebaker, which had workshops in South Bend, Indiana. On April 11, 1906, Chatelain, in order to improve his credentials as a dealer in transport equipment, wrote to Studebaker. His letter was very specific about the needs of the local transport industry and was therefore addressed to the manufacturers rather than to the company's sales agent in New York. He wanted an estimate for a wagon similar to one he had ordered in 1904 but with two-and-a-half-inch concord steel axles capable of withstanding encounters with tree stumps, rocks, and termite hills. A wagon that Chatelain had previously bought from California had only had one-and-a-half-inch axles, which had not proved robust enough. Wagons from Portugal, although competitively priced, were not as sturdy as the ones developed in America for the transcontinental wagon trails. The Indiana Studebaker was equipped with wheels five inches thick and had massive rear-screw brakes. For the African trade the bed of each wagon had to be sixteen feet long with sideboards two-and-a-half inches thick. Chatelain wanted his wagons equipped with side boxes rather than a high front box and with twenty yokes and twenty sets of ox chains instead of the more usual ten yokes supplied for work on the American plains.

Chatelain had not been satisfied with his first Studebaker purchase. That wagon had broken down three days out of Benguela. Its sideboards had cracked under heavy loads on steep trails and its paint had peeled in the tropical sun. Chatelain, who had sold the wagon on credit, had been forced to grant his customer a discount for poor workmanship, and the invoice had remained long in dispute. Despite his diminished profit margin on this first order, Chatelain hoped that if he placed regular orders Studebaker might offer him favorable terms. Competition in the wagon trade was growing, and a Cape Town firm of wagon builders had established an agency in Benguela and poached two of Chatelain's customers. Equally worrying was the rumor that the firm of Marques Pires and Company had acquired exclusive rights to the sale of any Studebaker landed at Benguela. Chatelain pointed out to his Indiana correspondent that Marques Pires did not have a good reputation and he therefore hoped that Studebaker would continue to supply the mission with high-class wagons.

Some of the larger sums in Chatelain's business accounts concern the trade not only in wagons but also in oxen. The station sometimes held sixty or more bullocks and oxen on its land as well as its ten cows and an assortment of goats, sheep, ducks, hens, and pigeons. On February 5, 1906, Chatelain wrote in Afrikaans to Susanna Behan, a widowed neighbor, about payments she owed him on six oxen that were worth 210 milreis. Such a sum, he said, was too large to be entrusted to an "ordinary Kaffir," so he suggested that she make the payment to the Benguela Railway Company and ask the company office to issue her a money order, which she could safely send by messenger. Still the debt was not paid, and Chatelain had constant cause to grumble about the large sums his clients owed him. He maintained close social contacts with his neighbors and spoke fluent Afrikaans, but credit was a slippery business and on one frustrated occasion he wrote that a "Boer's word of honour is as tangible as the wind." Relations with his Swiss colleagues were not always harmonious either, and he had difficulty recruiting catechists and artisans willing to turn their hand to any task, however menial. Alfred Balmer, with help from casual black laborers, did much of the station's plowing, hoeing, weeding, and harvesting. Ali Pieren, who was more mechanically inclined, serviced, repaired, and improved the water wheel that drove the corn mill. On one memorable morning the Swiss farmhands were thrilled to see the mill doing 82 revolutions per minute. They hoped that with more rain to fill the millstream they might achieve 100 revolutions and grind one whole sack of meal each day. Frederic Leuba, the most intellectual of the mission staff, wrote poetry, fiction, and plays when not engaged in heavy farm work. The temperamental mission lad, Girod, was a trial to his elders and was liable to beat laborers who displeased him, a colonial practice that the mission aspired to eradicate.

Chatelain was also the district pharmacist and a medical adviser with a cosmopolitan clientele on the highland. When Apollinario Pereira wrote that he was feeling ill, Chatelain diagnosed a poor condition of the liver and sold him two mild types of purgative. One was a powder also used by menopausal women; the other was a liquid, of which he was to take 30 drops along with a dose of the powder, wrapped in fine paper and swallowed like a pill, the treatment to be repeated daily as necessary. He also recommended that Mr. Pereira take quinine and sent him a flask of good-quality quinine powder, for which he charged 2,000 reis. He recommended four or five measures of quinine per day until the fever subsided and then one a day for a week afterwards. It was not only local Portuguese who consulted Chatelain about their ailments. When Mr. Wilde, at the Benguela railhead, thought he had a tapeworm, Chatelain told him to eat nothing but bread and milk for a whole day and then, on an empty stomach, to take the powder that Chatelain sold him. He also recommended a strong dose of Epsom salts and a diet of pumpkin seeds. If his spleen was the cause of the problem, he was to take bottled medicine three times a day and rub ointment on the pain before wrapping himself in a warm bandage. For good measure Chatelain also sold his patient some antidyspepsia tablets to be taken twice daily before meals. Another client, the widow Behan who had so chronically failed to pay for her oxen, was also a patient of the mission. Although Chatelain did not succeed in curing her husband of his chronic syphilis, he was able to treat the widow so effectively that she lived on to marry again. On such amateur foundations was the great Swiss hospital at Kalukembe founded.

Chatelain was also the district photographer. He developed film for other missions and took portrait photographs of local personalities. In January 1906 he at last found the time and materials to develop and print a batch of seventy-two photographs of life on the Caconda plateau. In 1897 he had captured his first meeting with the elders of Kalukembe on film, and ten years later many of them were still his friends and neighbors. One picture showed the all-important mission warehouse, with his own bedroom, office, and pharmacy on the upper storey. He photographed a South African prospector with a Welsh assistant who passed through with their pack mules. He photographed the commandant of the local fortress with his slave concubine and their tame monkey. Chatelain took pictures of clay potters, of water carriers, of women threshing wheat and pounding corn, of men drinking beer and taking snuff, of chiefs and kings posing with their stool bearers, of a hunter with a valuable white seashell on his wig, of girls wearing strings of beads and leg rings. Pictures of Boer houses and wagons were accompanied by pictures of a "Bushman" mother, captured in the Kalahari, raising children fathered by a native Boer drover. The village also had four "Hottentot" drovers brought up from Damaraland. One fifteen-year-old Boer woman whom Chatelain met was married to a Portuguese Jew from Morocco. He also photographed a young Boer widow with several children who possessed her own Studebaker wagon, ordered, Chatelain mentioned regretfully, from the factory in America rather than through his mission agency. When making photographs for Otto Wilde of the Benguela Railway, the photographer charged two milreis for six paper prints, or a little more for those printed as postcards. One picture taken with his camera was of Chatelain himself, wearing his three-piece suit with the gold watch chain—recalling his youth in the watchmaking canton of Neuchâtel in Switzerland—and a large-brimmed hat.

Chatelain also traded in firearms. When touring the plateau buying maize, beans, sweet potatoes, and cassava to feed the mission or sell to the colonial administration, he paid with gunpowder and gun flints stocked in his traveling bazaar. The mission itself was poorly equipped with hunting guns but did possess one Winchester. Attempts to make their own cartridges for such a modern weapon nearly led to the death of both Chatelain and his assistant. When they tried to remove a jammed cartridge, it exploded and made Chatelain temporarily deaf. He asked that the next Swiss worker coming out to Africa bring with him 500 manufactured cartridges, though clearing war materials through Portuguese customs was to prove difficult. Good-quality guns using cartridges were a major item sold by the bush traders in Angola. From 1899, however, foreigners such as the Swiss and the Boers needed a government license before they could hold such weapons, and Chatelain spent much effort obtaining the necessary documents for his customers. Some of the modern guns being sold in 1906 were old breech-loaders left over from the American Civil War. The trade guns sold to the natives, by contrast, were ancient muzzle-loading muskets, which could be sold in huge numbers without a license. These ubiquitous guns provided the traders with good profits on the sale of loose gunpowder to be poured down the barrel. Musket balls were made by local artisans to suit the needs of both warfare and hunting. Muzzle-loaders were not very effective in elephant hunting, and much of the ivory trade gradually fell into the hands of Boers who used high-velocity rifles to kill their prey and then carried their trophies to the coast on ox wagons. Muzzle-loaders were, however, useful to slave raiders or caravan guards who herded captives along the trade paths to the ports. Only in 1913, after international pressure had curtailed the sale of captives, was the trade in loose gunpowder outlawed. The administration simultaneously confiscated a quarter of a million guns held in native hands.

Social disruption in early colonial Angola was fueled as much by the ubiquitous sale of cheap rum as by the sale of muzzle-loaders. Chatelain steadfastly refused to trade in alcohol and preached vainly against the lack of sobriety all around. The trade in wine and rum, together with the equally addictive trade in tobacco and snuff, was the mainstay of trading posts scattered across the Caconda highland, but Chatelain refused to allow such commodities on his premises. He accepted that his staff surreptitiously smoked tobacco, and he was even told that one of his expatriate employees sold rum behind his back, but the mission store refrained from dealing with chiefs who could be induced to sell cattle for as little as a couple of bottles of rum per bullock. Tobacco did become a bone of contention between moralizing missionaries and struggling merchants. In the days of the Brazilian slave trade, tobacco had been a key currency commodity used for trading transactions and wage payments. In the twentieth century tobacco was one of the crops that the Portuguese administration would have liked to grow in Angola, after the British success in growing it in Zimbabwe and Malawi. The tobacco industry, however, did not take root in Angola, and settlers improbably blamed the missions. The missionaries' moral scruples, it was said, had so infected the peasant population that Angolans refused to buy, plant, or sell tobacco. Such a belief in the power of the missions would have astonished Chatelain. The idea that mission morality, rather than good, rational African business sense, had discouraged black farmers from growing tobacco was based on growing Portuguese xenophobia. By the early twentieth century this xenophobia was shared by the cultured Portuguese members of colonial high society who had once been Chatelain's intimate friends, as well as by petty-minded administrators and isolated traders in the bush.

The Swiss mission campaigned in vain against the widespread abuse of alcohol and tobacco, but its primary raison d'être was to stem the practice of slavery. Slave owning remained almost universal in the early twentieth century, as Chatelain was constantly reminded, and virtually all his Boer customers were slave holders. In May 1906 he was woken one morning before dawn by cries of distress coming from his compound. Under cover of darkness the son of Jan Vermaak, a local Boer settler, had ridden over to the mission with two black employees, one a Kwamato and the other a Nganguela, and stealthily entered the compound to seize a woman whom he claimed to be his slave. To stop the woman from screaming, Vermaak had hit her so hard that she fell as though dead, with a large head wound. His men tied her up and were attempting to carry her off when the alarm was raised by women in neighboring sleeping quarters. Chatelain, in Afrikaans, informed young Vermaak that slavery was no longer accepted under Portuguese colonial law. The woman turned out to be a Luba from Katanga who had been captured by rebel soldiers in Leopold's Congo and sold to a black slave trader from Bihé. She was then caught up in the Huambo War and captured as a war trophy by a Portuguese soldier, who sold her to a white dealer. He in turn sold her for cash to Vermaak senior, from whose compound she had fled to seek refuge in the mission. Prevented from recovering her, young Vermaak threatened to call up the Boer commando unit and have the interfering wagon dealer assassinated. Chatelain reported the incident to the district commissioner at Caconda, pointing out that the 1890 Brussels Conference Act, to which Portugal was party, outlawed Angola's slave trade and that the act required the commissioner to punish anyone holding slaves within Portuguese territory. This was the third time, Chatelain said, that Boers had tried to kidnap people from the mission claiming them to be their legally owned slaves.

Chatelain's protest about the illegality of slave holding generated hostility among some of his best customers and closest neighbors, who resented the refuge given by the mission to abused natives who had escaped their masters. One such refugee was a child called Domingo, who arrived at the station one Sunday morning during the hour of worship. His father was a goldsmith who had moved with his son from Luanda to Benguela and had bought a female slave as his concubine. When Domingo was about six years old, his father died and his aunt, not knowing what to do with him, gave him to the Belgian trading agency in the town. The Casa Belga apparently sold him to a Belgian planter, Raes, who had married a Boer widow and settled on the Caconda plateau. Raes had a particularly violent reputation—it was said that he had killed one of his black mistresses and burned her hut to hide the evidence—but it was his wife who took to beating young Domingo with a hippopotamus-hide whip when she was displeased with the performance of his domestic duties. When the brutalized child arrived at the Swiss mission, Raes flew into such a rage that he threatened to kill Chatelain. He reminded him that Lincoln, after whom the Swiss mission was named, had been murdered for freeing slaves. Raes warned him that within a year there would be nothing left of the Swiss station but smoldering ashes. Since both Raes and his wife owed significant trading debts to the Swiss store, burning the mission account books might have been financially advantageous to them. Chatelain handed young Domingo over to the district commissioner at Caconda. There, however, the only justice he received was another beating to deter him from running away again. Such beatings were normal, as one slave holder explained to the investigative journalist Henry Nevinson. It was his practice, he said, to flog any escapee very soundly for a first offense and, if he or she tried to escape a second time, to sell the escapee immediately to a slave dealer.[3] Once shipped to the island plantations of São Tomé, a slave would have no chance of escape. The fate of little Domingo after the authorities had returned him to his Belgian owner is not recorded.

One of the horrors experienced in slave-owning societies was the physical exploitation of defenseless women, who had no right to privacy or protection from unbridled male lust. Abuses that had been rife in the slave-based Roman empire of southern Europe, the Arab empire of the Near East, and the Hispanic empire of the Americas survived into the twentieth century in the Portuguese empire in Africa. Chatelain, himself a confirmed bachelor, began only slowly to recognize the corrosion that colonial sexual practices brought to the highland society in which he lived. He worried that his Swiss colleagues might, unlike himself, fall under the tempting influence of the unmarried girls who lived at the station. More seriously, he worried that when he hired out his Swiss craftsmen to work in the encampments of English railway engineers and mineral prospectors, they might adopt the colonial custom of inviting young slave concubines to share their cabins. His letters to his sister, who became his main confidante after the deaths of his mother and grandmother, are full of forebodings about the ubiquitous temptations of tobacco, alcohol, and above all sexual immorality. He was particularly disturbed by the behavior of one mission-educated adolescent who offered her sexual services to an engineer who camped near the mission while installing a telegraph cable up to Caconda from the coast. The young "whore" was a protégée of a former colleague and Chatelain felt himself in loco parentis, yet he was deeply reluctant to condone her behavior or receive her back at the station when her white lover repudiated her to move on up the telegraph line.

The ubiquitous exploitation of black people by white rulers caused Chatelain almost as much grief as drunkenness. Chatelain had known Commissioner Valdez since Valdez had arrived in Luanda as a beardless youth embarking on a colonial career and Chatelain had been the cultured man-about-town whom every educated Portuguese liked to invite to dinner to entertain the guests. Twenty years later, when Valdez was transferred from his provincial posting at Caconda and his removal caravan passed in front of the mission, he barely stopped to pass the time of day with his old companion of city days. He was now a portly man with a grizzled beard who was carried in a hammock. Behind him another set of bearers carried another hammock containing his *mestiço* mistress, and behind her was a string of young black women whom Chatelain took to be the commissioner's harem. The coolness of the commissioner's greeting may have reflected the fact that Valdez, like many other Portuguese officers in the highlands, was in deep financial debt to Chatelain's country store. The exploitation practiced by expatriates in Angola in 1906 was not confined to the Roman-style opulence of the Portuguese proconsuls. The English were no better, in Chatelain's view, since they bought not only men to work in their copper mines by day but women to serve their pleasure by night.

One of the surprising revelations in Chatelain's letter books is how cosmopolitan the expatriate community on the Caconda plateau had become. When the fourth Swiss laborer, Girod, arrived at the mission station, he was accompanied by a German boy of eighteen whom he had met on the slow boat from Antwerp as it steamed down the entire African coast picking up deck passengers along the route and depositing them where jobs were available. The German boy, without any experience or qualifications, was hoping to make his living in Angola simply by virtue of being European. But 1906 was not a good year for adventurers. Work on the railway was not going well, the transport business was in such deep recession that Chatelain's wagons were traveling half empty, and Angola was full of footloose whites seeking their fortune. Most recently, four Boer brothers, all with wives, families, and wagon trains of oxen, had taken eight months to cross the thirstlands via Lake Ngami. Chatelain welcomed more Boer settlers, especially when they opened a new wagon trail to Benguela, and hoped they would enhance his business. Expectations of new English custom were disappointed, however, when it became clear that the Benguela railway would bypass Caconda and take a more northerly route to the interior via Huambo and Bihé. This disappointment was matched by the pain caused to Chatelain by wilder sorts of adventures like those of a brilliant, violent young Scottish aristocrat, Captain Cunningham, who had served the

British during their invasion of the Tranvaal and then managed to get himself murdered in the little Angolan kingdom of Kasanje during an unnecessary dispute over the price of goat's meat.

Although Chatelain spent much of his trading time dealing with foreigners and even, apparently, recruiting their contract laborers, he saw his main purpose in Angola as mission work. Others did not see him in quite that light. The Union Castle shipping line refused to grant the Swiss Mission Philafricaine, which had replaced the American League of Friends as Chantelain's prime sponsor, the 10 percent discount that it allowed to bona fide missionary passengers on its steamers. Chatelain wrote to the company giving the British and Foreign Bible Society as a reference that could certify that he had been selling Bibles in Angola for twenty years. Bibles and religious tracts were one of his commercial lines, and he wrote to other mission stations offering these in different qualities, colors, bindings, and letterings, always carefully stressing the price. His greatest difficulty was in obtaining religious tracts (other than the Psalms) in Angola's vernacular languages. His letters to the mission at Bailundu seemed to go astray when he ordered a catalogue of their Umbundu hymnbooks. If, he said plaintively, the missionaries were really too busy to deal with this Swiss request, he wondered if one of the mission ladies might reply to his letter. In his depressed isolation he even wondered how soon the new telegraph might reach the American mission and how much per word it would cost him to order his books by Morse code. He was not optimistic, however, remembering that in Luanda twenty years before, runners with cleft sticks delivered messages more quickly than the electric telegraph.

Chatelain was so meticulous about chasing up his trading debts, calculating his profits on corn milling and transport riding, and living a frugal life that toward the end of his career he could write to R. G. Moffat at the American station in Bihé that he had accumulated enough money to open a second Swiss station. The Mission Philafricaine would not, he admitted, finance a lifestyle comparable to that of an American missionary, but his own workers accepted a much more Spartan subsistence. The new Swiss mission, he said, was to be "self-helping," though not self supporting. It would have to be in a region in which it would be possible to trade in rubber, the only commodity that was both legitimate and profitable. The Lincoln station, he admitted, had so far made a loss on both cattle raising and agriculture. In 1906, when the rains were poor, Chatelain took cartloads of maize and beans to afflicted villages to sell in exchange for cattle, which he brought back to the mission, where water and fodder were still available. Despite his best efforts, however, no less than twenty large animals died of fever, as well as eighty goats. Chatelain's days were filled with tending sick but valuable animals, especially those he had sold on credit to customers who refused to pay for them until their survival was ensured. Under this stress the mission entrepreneur dreamt of using Lincoln as a stepping-stone to more promising and profitable regions in the deep interior.

Chatelain's Swiss business methods are clearly spelled out in his papers. His religious beliefs, by contrast, are something of a mystery. At Bishop Taylor's multidenominational mission in Luanda he was often intolerant of all but his Quaker colleagues. His relations with the churches in Switzerland were also complex, and he seems to have been linked neither to the theological school of the Free Church of Vaud nor to the established State Church of Vaud. His small support committee, in which the dominant figure was his sister (later his biographer), included a few ordained men, but it had no wide popular appeal. He corresponded with the Zion City religious community in America, which supplied him with a periodical called *Leaves of Healing*, and he hoped that his Boer customers would have their hearts healed by reading the Dutch edition. He particularly craved the healing prayers of Dr. Dowie of Zion City, Illinois. He considered it a miracle that despite his persistent fevers, rheumatism, consumption, catarrh, and nearsightedness, and a lifelong limp caused by one shortened leg and one stiff hip, he was still alive. His friends in America tried to persuade him to give up using drugs and to trust in faith healing, but when malarial delirium struck him down he never quite dared to give up quinine. These friends did not approve of his laying on of hands to cure illnesses, and Chatelain admitted that none of those whom he had cured had seriously repented of their sins. In addition to trying to eradicate drinking and smoking, he tried to discourage the eating of pork. Despite his piety, the devil still sent Chatelain "locusts, lice, jiggers, rats, mildew, drought, moths, rust, termites and cattle sickness which destroyed everything that rogues and burglars of every race had not already robbed." The Lincoln station, he told a correspondent in Zion City, was not exactly the lion's den, but it was full of serpents.

During his last year in Angola Chatelain became weary, confiding to C. E. Welsh that the missionary path was a stony one. Whenever an African trainee seemed ready to become a church member, he became puffed up and unruly. All too often, stealing and immorality forced Chatelain to dismiss his acolytes. Even when men did progress toward a Christian understanding, their wives pulled them back "into a semi-heathen state." Some of Chatelain's pupils were slaves who had run away from their Boer and Portuguese owners, but they were not grateful for the protection they had received and were unready, in his eyes, to join the church. Recruiting Europeans willing to accept Chatelain's austere standard of simple living was difficult, and he fell out with most of his expatriate followers, bitterly comparing some of them to Judas. Chatelain nonetheless dreamed of recruiting further mission workers that they might break the fetters of thousands of slaves and cause the whole colonial system to collapse.

Such subversive sentiments did not go unobserved in the Portuguese imperial administration, although Chatelain tried to be discreet in his comments about the political situation in Angola. In 1906, in a letter to Brother Welsh in America, he asked him not to publicize the letter or to speak of it except in very guarded terms. Persecution of Protestants was on the increase, and an American missionary in Bihé had been expelled. Worse still, missionaries of all nationalities were ordered to hand over any refugee slave who might be living in their compounds and to forbid entry to any new refugees who might have fled from their owners. Even more immediately, the district commissioner in Caconda informed Chatelain that all missions were forbidden to teach reading and writing to anyone, even household members living in the mission compounds. The authorities were particularly frightened of missionaries who taught literacy through the vernacular languages. Outraged, Chatelain appealed to higher authority against this form of persecution. He predicted that if such an incredible ban on education were to be applied to the Boers, who cherished the right to teach their own children in their own language, the ensuing violence would threaten the whole Portuguese presence in southern Angola.

Despite his desire to see the slave-trading system "totter and fall like the walls of Jericho," Chatelain was aware that imperial overrule by Portugal did provide him with some protection that he could ill afford to lose. Threats to the mission were a constant fact of life. Chatelain had been warned by several sympathizers about the possibility of his being poisoned. The fears that Chatelain might be murdered by his deeply indebted customers, or that his station might be burnt down to remove all traces of the monies that were owed to him, were not entirely fanciful. When Henry Nevinson followed the slave trail from Bailundu to Catumbela, he too feared that he might be murdered because of any publicity he might give to the practices of the slave traders. Chatelain read Nevinson's articles in *Harper's* magazine with great care and told his correspondents that as far as he could detect they were an entirely accurate record of the conduct of the slave trade. He himself remained anxious to protect his own position and avoid giving publicity to the crimes of the Portuguese.

The last years of the old Portuguese monarchy's imperial rule in Angola were characterized by a sense of impending doom. Everyone, Chatelain said, was expecting the revolution to break out in Lisbon, but the national finances of Portugal were in such a state that that the republicans were reluctant to take on the economic crises of the empire. One of Chatelain's friends from his Luanda days was a Freemason who gladly anticipated the sweeping away of the old Catholic order. A district commissioner appointed to Caconda in 1907 was also a covert Freemason, as he discreetly admitted to Chatelain, but his revolutionary credentials did not lead him to be lenient in the matter of petty regulations and mindless bureaucratic form filling. It was this plague of bureaucracy that finally drove Chatelain out of Angola. Shortly before he left, Chatelain traveled to Caconda to confront the district commissioner. The mission had been fined 25 milreis for illegally selling rum. Chatelain pointed out that this was preposterous since he was known to be a ferocious opponent of the rum trade. The commissioner explained that the fine was not for selling rum, but for failing to fill in tax returns for the months of January, February, and March 1907, in which he was expected to declare how much rum, if any, he had sold. Chatelain thereupon pointed out, with perfect logic, that the forms had only been issued in April and that it would therefore not have been possible for him to submit them in January, February, or March. The district tax collector resolutely refused to accept any excuses, and rather than face prison and the confiscation of his trading stock, Chatelain paid the fine. When he appealed to the provincial governor at Benguela, the fine was confirmed, and it gradually became clear to Chatelain that not only did the local authorities wish to drive him out of the highland, but the imperial authorities wished to drive him out of Angola. The governor-general in Luanda allegedly claimed that he had never heard of Chatelain or his Protestant trading station, but everyone else in the colonial establishment knew Chatelain, and many were pleased to see him go.

The Caconda district records, now somewhat water stained but safely housed in Angola's National Archive, reveal that the authorities were well aware that Chatelain had been publishing "defamatory" stories about Angola in the United States. His accounts of labor conditions were so damaging to Portuguese imperial pride that his removal was deemed desirable. The imperial government in Luanda, however, was more aware than any magistrate in the provinces that Chatelain was an internationally renowned personage and that any high-handed deportation might have even worse consequences than his journalistic activities. Hence the attempt to drive him out by legal chicanery and the use of bureaucratic forms that no one else had ever been required to complete. What neither the local magistrates nor the central government realized, however, was that Chatelain's subversive reports were sent not merely to Christian congregations in America but also to business houses in Europe. Portugal was about to be engulfed in a revolution with wide international ramifications. Before the storm broke, however, Chatelain sailed for Switzerland, and in 1908 he died in his bed in Lausanne.

5

The Case of Belgium and Portugal

Belgium and Portugal, the two small colonial powers in Africa, are not normally juxtaposed for comparative purposes. Instead the Belgian sphere is normally contrasted with the neighboring French colonies of equatorial Africa and the Portuguese sphere is seen to have more in common with the white-settler colonies of southern Africa. In this chapter, a longer version of which was originally published in French, it is shown that links and similarities between the two Roman Catholic imperial mini-nations are in fact illuminating. Both countries, for instance, had strong anticlerical traditions, which played significant roles in the empires, sometimes at the inspiration of Masonic lodges. Both modern empires were born in the trauma of 1908, when Belgium confiscated the Congo state from its Saxe-Coburg king, Leopold, while Portuguese revolutionaries assassinated their Saxe-Coburg king, Carlos, and introduced republicanism to their colonies. Thereafter the links and comparisons involve financial ties, attitudes to race, the management of plantation policies, the transport of industrial metals, and the marketing of gemstones.[1]

In the year 1908 the colonial empires in Central Africa underwent a severe crisis brought on by the growth of a humanitarian movement which challenged the way in which some European powers had disregarded the human rights of their colonial subjects. The forces behind the humanitarian protest included the press, the missionary churches, diplomats in consular services, and some members of the business community. The two prime targets of the outcry against excessive exploitation were the rich plantation island of São Tomé, administered under the authority of the Portuguese crown, and the struggling Congo state, personally ruled by the king of the Belgians. The transformation of both the Portuguese empire in Africa and the soon-to-be Belgian territories in Africa went hand in hand during the years 1908 and 1910. The repercussions of change and reform were felt not only in São Tomé and Congo, but also in Angola, the mainland colony from which São Tomé had been drawing most of its servile labor.

Of the two great colonial crises that brought the minor powers to world attention in the years preceding the First World War, the Congo crisis was the first to break. Leopold II of Saxe-Coburg, king of the Belgians and cousin to the royal houses of both Britain and Portugal, had had a long career in business adventures. The Congo "Free" State, which his commercial and military associates had carved out of the heart of Africa in the 1880s, was very much his personal fief. It was neither a free independent state, governed by its own people, nor a colony governed on behalf of the people of Belgium. The Belgian national exchequer did not provide any tax revenue to overcome the constant fiscal crises that afflicted the management of the king's African estates. In order to recover the costs of his personal investment in the colonial adventure, Leopold therefore rented out subcolonies to free-enterprise corporations, which paid him a license fee in return for an unfettered hand in extracting natural wealth and exploiting human resources. The king also retained a crown domain under his personal control. The king's soldiers, administrators, and traders were of mixed national origin, coming from Britain, Scandinavia, and America as well as from Belgium. The best-known, not to say most notorious, of Leopold's associates was the Welshborn American journalist Henry Morton Stanley, who, after "discovering" Livingstone, had used the firepower of his modern rifles to shoot his way across Africa and down the Congo River to the Atlantic. Another of Leopold's powerful agents was the great Swahili slave hunter Tippu Tip, whose domains in eastern Congo became part of Leopold's fief. The king assured the international community that his objectives were humane and that he aimed to suppress, rather than encourage, the capturing of slaves in Central Africa. The violent methods practiced by Stanley and Tippu Tip nevertheless survived under Leopold's rule.

The Congo crisis of 1908 arose essentially because Leopold, after twenty years of effort, found it increasingly difficult to meet the cost of administering his territory. Profits for himself and his associates were extracted by the tactics of coercion and kidnapping that had been brought into the Congo by earlier Christian and Muslim slave catchers from Angola in the west and from Zanzibar in the east. Leopold's agents also used violent compulsion to force villagers into the dangerous pursuit of ivory elephants, thus emulating the armed gangs of "Turkish" ivory traders from Egypt who terrorized the populations of northern Congo. The kidnapping of women and children, who were then held prisoner until their male relatives had hunted enough ivory to pay a suitable ransom, was officially condemned but covertly practiced by the Leopoldian state. As ivory, confined to the most inaccessible heartlands of the continent, became scarce, violence rose to new heights. New terror was added to the Leopoldian system of extraction when rubber was recognized as a valuable Congo resource.

In the late nineteenth century the motor industry and electrical industry began to create a demand for wild rubber with which to manufacture vehicle tires and insulate copper cables. Leopold's agents found that rubber could be tapped in the deep equatorial forest. They drove not only men but women and children to explore the most dangerous recesses of the wilderness in search of any plant, creeper, or root that could yield rubber. At first the agents made easy profits, but by the turn of the century the price of rubber began to fall as regular plantations were established in Southeast Asia and Latin America. Leopold's revenue shrank and his agents pressed their conscripts to travel ever deeper into the forests to bring ever more rubber to the riverside depots. Villagers who failed to meet the quota arbitrarily imposed on them were severely beaten. In the extreme cases that brought the Congo to world attention, collectors who failed to find surviving rubber-yielding plants were viciously mutilated. Hands were publicly amputated, spreading mortal dread among the foragers and forcing them to neglect their family crops in a desperate search to find rubber or be maimed for life. These Congo atrocities were brought to light and given credence by the British consul in Congo, Roger Casement. A Congo Reform Movement successfully mobilized international opinion against the tyrannical exploitations that Leopold had failed to curb. In 1908 the Belgian parliament decided that the king was not a fit person to be entrusted with a colony and Congo was annexed by the government to become the Belgian Congo. Thereafter a European ministry rather than a royal entrepreneur was the ultimate arbiter of colonial affairs. The extraction of colonial wealth continued, but a minimal level of supervision was introduced.

The Portuguese dimension to the colonial crisis of 1908 was in some respects similar to the Belgian one. The colony of Angola had been carved out of Central Africa by Portuguese soldiers in the last quarter of the nineteenth century, just as the Congo state had been carved out of adjacent territory by Leopold's mercenaries. To make the territory economically self-financing, conscripts were forced to clear footpaths so that long-distance caravans to the interior could fetch rubber and ivory gathered under conditions that were probably little better than those imposed on the conquered peoples of Congo. Unwilling porters, underpaid and underfed, constantly tried to flee from their harsh servitude. Some found refuge in stockaded havens built by kingdoms that resisted colonial domination, and others sought protection in mission stations that helped them to escape from a life that was little better than slavery. The invading colonials used armed force to recapture runaway conscripts as though they were slaves. African resistance, however, created such difficulty in establishing a plantation economy in Angola that Portugal preferred to revitalize the old plantation complex on the offshore islands of São Tomé and Príncipe. Their policy restored the export trade of slaves shipped out of Angola.

The revival of the plantations on São Tomé was based on a change from coffee growing in the highland to cocoa growing on the warmer slopes of the islands. At their height the plantations employed 40,000 workers and needed to import about 4,000 new ones each year to replace those who died of exhaustion, disease, or despair. The majority were slaves who had been captured in the far interior of Central Africa, brought to the Atlantic coast in gangs chained together with wooden shackles, and sold to dealers who shipped them to the islands. Nominally each slave was freed before embarkation and issued a contract to serve on a plantation for a fixed term of five years. In practice no worker ever returned to mainland Africa. The opportunities for escape and even survival were limited since the islands had neither hospitable chiefs nor sympathetic missionaries to shelter the victims of abuse. At the end of each five-year period survivors were automatically assumed, without consultation, to have enrolled for a further five years.

The abuses in the Atlantic colonies became so notorious that Portugal feared that without minimal reform it would find its colonies subjected to confiscation like those of King Leopold. This fear was not entirely illusory. Another member of the Saxe-Coburg family became involved in the reshaping of Africa in the years preceding the First World War. Kaiser Wilhelm of Germany, the grandson of Queen Victoria of England, may not have been closely involved in his government's confidential diplomacy, but his chancellery did aspire to partition the colonies of Portugal. It was aided by the connivance of Great Britain, where a negative appreciation of Portugal's colonial practices was widely publicized by the journalist Henry Nevinson in his articles on the "modern slavery" of Angola. Portugal's standing as an imperial power was further damaged in 1908 by the assassination of King Carlos, the member of the Saxe-Coburg family who reigned in

Lisbon. Two years later his son was driven into exile by a conspiracy of anarchists and republicans, and thereafter the way was open for Britain and Germany to plot the partition of the Portuguese empire. Their plan was simple. Southern Angola, adjacent to German Namibia, and northern Mozambique, adjacent to German Tanzania, would be handed to Germany on the ground that the Portuguese administration was incapable of dealing efficiently with the needs of modern business entrepreneurs. Britain would then help itself to the remainder of the two territories. Portugal responded to the threat by sending one of its most robust republican politicians, General Norton de Matos, to Angola as a high commissioner with a virtually dictatorial free hand. Norton was forced by foreign opinion to moderate some traditional abuses, and Angolan workers sold on contract to the cocoa islands were henceforth allowed to return home after ten years' service, a reform proposed in 1908 but intemperately rejected by the then-royal government of Portugal as an impertinent attempt by Britain to interfere with its proud sovereign autonomy. But the republicans wasted no time in finding new methods of extracting service from the huge mainland provinces that they had inherited in Angola. Norton began, in particular, to conscript women into forced labor gangs to build a network of earth roads that would meet the needs of the newly introduced automobiles and trucks.

Transport was one problem faced by all colonizers in Central Africa; King Leopold himself recognized it as the essence of colonizing. The Congo faced particular problems in that its richest mineral deposits, the ones requiring the heaviest machinery and producing the bulkiest exports, were in Katanga, a thousand miles from any seaport. The shortest route to the sea led across Lake Tanganyika, through German East Africa, and down to the traditional but remote and not very convenient old Swahili port of Dar es Salaam. An alternative "national" route to the western sea ran through Belgian territory but involved the use of several railways linked by stretches of navigable river, thus requiring multiple trans-shipments. A longer but more continuous route to the sea wended its way across several boundaries and over the

Zambezi bridge to South Africa's remote ports. To overcome the handicaps British investors designed a short route that would lead out of Katanga, across the Angola plateau, and down to the Atlantic at Benguela, where a deep-water harbor could be built at Lobito Bay. This Benguela railway was not completed until the 1920s, but from then until its destruction in the 1970s it was one of the key arteries of Africa, carrying Congo minerals to a deep-sea port.

Carrying minerals from the Belgian mines could never be as profitable as extracting them from Portuguese territory. The centuries-old search for minerals in Angola, however, had never produced great bounty. Despite bitter wars over mineral rights fought between Portugal and Africa's old Atlantic kingdoms, only small quantities of copper had ever been found. In the eighteenth century a Basque-run iron foundry was built by a Portuguese dictator, the marquis of Pombal, on the site of the old mines of the Ndongo kingdom, but the ambitious venture proved abortive. In the twentieth century an expensive railway was built to open iron mines in Angola's deep south, but they failed when the price of ore collapsed. The one success in mineral extraction began in the 1920s when Angola discovered good-quality gem diamonds for the jewelry trade. The diamond fields were staked out in newly conquered territories in the northeast of the colony. A semiclosed concessionary territory was defined, financed, and administered by an extraction company linked to Britain, Belgium, and South Africa. A marketing cartel controlled by De Beers ensured that Portugal obtained good prices for Angola's gems on the highly regulated diamond market. The Lunda-speaking peoples of the northeast became the captive subjects of a state-within-the-state. They were compelled to serve long tours of duty in the open-cast mines and were held under closed conditions designed to limit pilferage. Under the authoritarian regime that governed Portugal between 1926 and 1974, this remote colonial mining complex became an enclave of expatriate exiles to which some dissident Portuguese engineers were banished as punishment for their liberal views. By the time the fascist-style regime fell, another mineral enclave had been opened up in Angola's offshore oil field of Cabinda. This too was under foreign control, though the capital and technology came from America rather than Belgium. In the 1960s oil outstripped diamonds as Angola's main mineral export. Diamonds, however, made a comeback of considerable political significance during the wars that followed Angola's independence. Some of the old diamond diggings, and many new ones, fell into the hands of rebel forces in the 1980s. These rebels smuggled their diamonds out through Congo marketing rings to pay for their supplies of food, fuel, and weapons.

In Angola minerals became the dominant export only after independence. In the Belgian Congo, by contrast, mining was important from the colonial outset. Congo mined large quantities of industrial diamonds along the rivers downstream from Angola's fields of gemstones. It also developed significant gold washing in the muddy streams of the eastern zones. Diamonds and gold both required the conscription of large numbers of subjects who were compelled to work under harsh conditions. Despite the glitter of diamonds and gold, the Belgian colonial economy became primarily dependent on industrial metals rather than rare minerals. The Congo copper mines in Katanga became the basis of the largest industrial complex in tropical Africa. The new industrial society incorporated an African workforce that became semiskilled and permanently urbanized. The miners of Katanga, unlike most colonial miners, did not form an all-male community of migrants whose economic and cultural roots remained in the countryside, but became a stabilized proletariat dependent on its wages. This Congo proletariat reproduced itself within the industrial complex, but Belgian policy did not allow these urban Africans to move far up the ladder of skill and opportunity, though it did give them significantly more literacy and technical competence than was available in Portugal's empire. Management, however, remained firmly in white hands. In between Katanga's white managers and the black workers a commercial class of expatriates included a service community from Greece. Elsewhere in Congo services and retail trading were often in the hands of Indian shopkeepers in the north and Portuguese artisans in the west.

One question in colonial history concerns the extent to which the formation of classes was influenced by racial attitudes. In the Belgian Congo, where mining and manufacturing saw the growth of a significant urban population, social mobility was hindered in two ways: first, and most obviously, by the white population's reserving for itself many of the tasks that carried status and a generous salary. The second way in which class formation was hindered, intentionally or unintentionally, was by the dividing of the African population into ethnic groups. Belgian policy on ethnicity fluctuated. Sometimes ethnic groups were seen as a safe means of dividing the native population into small segments that could be easily controlled. At other times policy favored the mixing of peoples so that no large block of workers—with an autonomous ethnic solidarity—might emerge.

The development of a stabilized labor force occurred at different times in the different regions of the Belgian Congo. Temporary labor camps initially had poor housing, poor sanitation, limited water supplies, and high levels of mortality. In sparsely populated Katanga the recruitment of labor was difficult, but the profits on mining were sufficient for companies to improve living conditions from the 1920s and so form a working-class core of employees supplemented by temporary migrant laborers. Industrial workers in the Belgian Congo gained craft skills and responsibilities that were not entrusted to Africans in the Rhodesias or South Africa. As a result they worked more effectively and so enhanced the profits of their imperial employers. The medical services provided for the stabilized workforce were improved, but mortality remained high among casual and migrant laborers. As the permanently urbanized workforce grew, the methods of social control changed. Instead of the brutal personal violence that rained down on early colonial workers, new forms of group organization were manipulated by the mining companies. They coopted the assistance of Catholic missions in creating "boy scout" solidarity and discipline within the work gangs. Social engineering was so pervasive that missions arranged marriages for urban employees by bringing brides to the city from appropriate ethnic communities. When paternalism failed, however, company managers quickly turned to violent repression. The Katanga mine strike of 1941 led to forty-eight men being shot and killed and many more wounded.

The Congo employees who came closest to forming a social class were the clerical workers, some of whom became leaders of political movements in the last years before independence. Clerical workers were divided, however, as to whether they should be the spokespersons of African society as a whole or should concentrate on the protecting of their own semiprivileged status in the colonial world, located midway between the white artisans and the black proletariat. Members of the black secretarial class were known as the *évolués*. Their ambivalent attitudes fluctuated between collaboration and protest, between enjoying salaries with status and resenting the disdain they suffered at the hands of petty white supervisors. In Belgium even liberal-minded politicians and working-class socialists did not have much sympathy toward upwardly mobile black aspirations. Racial prejudice was so strong in Congo that black resentment became the driving force behind the 1950s radicalization of colonial politics. Racial antagonism, however, was not the only emotive force to reach fever pitch in late colonial Congo, and ethnic fragmentation was the harbinger of the violent confrontations of decolonization and its postcolonial aftermath. The utopian aspirations and bitter social disappointments of Belgium's colonial subjects led to half a decade of confrontation after 1960 as the large and apparently powerful empire that the Belgians had built around their financial and industrial interests crumbled. From the ashes, however, the key institutions of colonialism—the army, the church, and the mines—were to recover their authority.

Mining, as the central activity of colonial enterprise in Congo, had wide repercussions on rural society. Despite anxious resistance, labor recruiters and food procurers reached and transformed many diverse, distinct, and remote farming communities. Villages were broken up and their inhabitants resettled along lines of road, river, and rail communication. Peasants were set to work on plantations where local crops were grown to feed miners with their accustomed diet. Compulsion and punishment remained the constant refrain after the Belgian annexation of Congo, even if the extreme horrors of mutilation had been replaced by the lash. Slow working practices may have been the result of poor incentives and inadequate nutrition, but disease also spread lethargy through the newly concentrated communities. Health officials had to learn that moving workers from one disease environment to another could have serious consequences on mortality rates in compounds. Psychiatric illness also affected colonial subjects who had been captured, roped together, and marched away in terrified columns. In semideserted villages the catastrophe of colonialism was often attributed to witchcraft. As communities became divided against themselves, misery, poverty, and recrimination spread. When the villages could no longer supply the mines with food, the Belgians opened up new-style colonial plantations.

The old colonial world had been dominated by planters, who often preferred to settle on tropical islands and relied on slave labor to produce their cotton, sugar, and tobacco. In the twentieth century some colonial powers adopted a rather different policy. Instead of moving people to islands, they conquered whole communities on the African mainland and forcibly encouraged local farmers to grow crops chosen by colonizers. These crops were not necessarily ones that would bring farmers good profits, but they provided colonizers with viable internal or export markets. The incentives used by Belgium as well as Portugal to change peasant practices involved only limited economic rewards alongside the compulsion used in agricultural policy. On traditional plantations laborers were more or less unwillingly conscripted to work for wages that did little to compensate them for their loss of freedom and the denial of their right to make rational economic choices in their agrarian strategies. Where plantations were not established, African farmers were compelled to grow crops on their own land, using their own families as labor, according to choices made by a commissioner or governor. The colonizers of Portuguese East Africa drew their revenue from sisal, coconut, sugar, and rice; in Portuguese West Africa and the Belgian Congo, where these crops were not viable, the main crops were coffee, maize, and palm oil. The most controversial crop in all areas, however, was cotton (see discussion below).

Each of the colonial crops had a distinctive effect on conquered societies. This effect was partly influenced by money, the introduction of which into rural society was one of the most far-reaching of the changes brought by colonization. In Congo the change from barter to coinage began soon after the ending of the Leopoldian system of extortion, when money was introduced to pay villagers for crops. The colonizers did not build a balanced economy based on consumer supply and demand, and cash did not long remain in peasant hands. Instead the new colonial coins were soon clawed back in taxation, which was intended not to pay for welfare services but rather to compel farmers to earn cash by growing colonial export crops. During the First World War the system was used to feed Belgian colonial troops sent to invade the German territories of Rwanda and Burundi on the Great Lake fringes of Congo. As colonial rule became entrenched, agricultural companies were set up to produce or process tropical crops. Palm oil production came to be dominated by the Unilever corporation, while peasant-grown cotton was processed by a state-run company. State intervention increased during the world Depression of the 1930s, and compulsory crop growing replaced the free-market and cooperative initiatives. Buying agencies became accustomed to purchasing crops at little more than a quarter of their free-market price. The state encouraged such extortion by building feeder roads that channeled cheap crops to the railway yards by truck. Not until the very end of the colonial period did an African productive class emerge that could buy land, select markets, and respond sensitively to a choice of economic opportunities. Protests about compulsion and an absence of free incentive had been the hallmarks of Congo farming in the Belgian period.

Colonial farming in Angola bore some similarities to Belgian agriculture in Congo. Indeed, some of the capital that was invested in Angolan plantations was Belgian, and some of the farmland that was used to grow colonial crops straddled the Atlantic railway linking Congo to Benguela. Angola's most important crop, however, was coffee grown in the north, where it had been introduced by Brazilian traders in the nineteenth century. The first "prototype" plantations used slave labor supervised by white convicts. Similar estates momentarily achieved a high level of prosperity in the 1890s, when accessible fertile land was violently seized from its African owners.[2] Production soon declined, however, when epidemics of smallpox and sleeping sickness devastated northern Angola, spread across the region by columns of conscript porters hired not only by Portugal and Belgium but by French colonizers on the north bank of the Congo River. Once the epidemics had burned themselves out, returning colonial farmers attempted to diversify their production and avoid dependence on a single crop in a restricted zone. Sugar cane was planted on the south coast of Angola, and when distilled as rum it sometimes gave an adequate return. When failure occurred, however, the industry came to be dominated by Portugal's colonial bank, which reluctantly acquired many sugar estates in exchange for bad debts. Another innovation was sisal, brought by German migrants who left Tanzania after the First World War and established plantations on the dry edges of the Angolan highlands. In the wetter lowlands Portuguese settlers developed palm oil plantations in the hope that palm oil would compete in price, if not in quality, with the olive oil produced by Portugal itself. A later form of oil-seed production was attempted with the cultivation of sunflowers. A further diversification was cattle ranching, introduced with limited regard for the land rights of the indigenous population. The crop that caused the greatest distress, however, and the one that triggered off an anticolonial rebellion, was cotton. Already in 1945 compulsory cotton growing was reported to be causing peasants to neglect their food crops to such an extent that serious famine had spread across central Angola. The dictators of Portugal, Prime Minister Salazar and his colonial minister Caetano, refused to heed the warnings of their local advisers, and the compulsory growing of cotton on poor, dry land continued until the end of the colonial period.

Both of the small colonial powers in tropical Africa were officially Roman Catholic when they began their colonizing practices. In Congo the Catholic Church came to be an important institution among the industrial workforce. The church enhanced obedience, discipline, and African acceptance of colonial hierarchy and authority. The Portuguese Catholic Church had a similar role in Angola, where it was seen as the church of the white expatriates and settlers rather than of the common people. Curiously, however, in both imperial nations there was also strong antagonism to the church, which was sometimes reflected in the attitudes of colonizers. In Belgium an anticlerical freemasonry was one significant strand of middle-class opposition to the dominance of the church. In French-speaking areas of Belgium there was also a working-class socialism that had atheistic tendencies. In Portugal the socialism was more muted, but the republican ideology that dominated the country for a generation after 1910 was strongly anticlerical, and many of the republican leaders were anti-Catholic Freemasons. The greatest antagonism to the established colonial church hierarchy came, however, from foreign missions run by Protestants who had no loyalty to the colonial metropolis (see chapter 3).

One of the earliest of the Protestant mission churches to take root in West Central Africa was the Baptist church from Britain, which became a dominant religious, educational, and cultural force in both Congo and Angola. Missionaries were seen by many as the handmaids of colonization, instilling a respect for European culture and an obedience to Christian doctrine that facilitated governance by white foreigners. The missions in Africa did some of the work that in Europe was being undertaken by progressive states, providing schools and hospitals for those who could not afford to pay privately for medicine or education. Yet while better health and better skills made colonization more profitable, mission activities were not always to the liking of colonial administrators. The missions accepted the need for obedience to the state, but they did not instill unalloyed Belgian or Portuguese patriotism into their congregations. When protest broke out against harsh forms of colonial exploitation, administrators tended to blame missionaries for fomenting rebellion. Although the Portuguese were offended by the liberalism of Protestants, they did not wish to offend Great Britain and allowed them to evangelize. The Portuguese church was too poor, and until 1926 too persecuted, to recruit missionaries of its own who might entrench Portuguese values in the tropics by teaching and precept. The Portuguese state therefore relied on foreign-funded missions, Catholic as well as Protestant. In south Angola much proselytizing was undertaken by Holy Ghost fathers from France.

In the Belgian section of the lower Congo region the Baptist Church was caught in the same trap as the missionaries in Angola. Baptist missionaries were dependent on the state for their preaching licenses, but they did not approve of colonial profiteering at the expense of African workers. Subversion took hold among Baptist congregations, and one African preacher, Simon Kimbangu, began to speak of the rights of black peoples and even of the power of Christ to speak to Africans unaided by white intermediaries. Kimbangu was rapidly captured and imprisoned, but his message could not be quelled. Although confined to a remote region of eastern Congo, his followers remembered him, and their number multiplied in the west. Small independent Kimbanguist churches sprang up in Angola as well as in Congo, and in the 1950s the prophet's son took command of the new far-reaching church. Eventually the Kimbanguist church, freed from the trammels of the state and independent of any white theological influence, was invited to become a full member of the World Council of Churches at Geneva.

Carried by new missions, fundamentalist Protestant traditions took root and spread to villages that had not been touched by the Flemish Catholic fathers or British Baptist pastors. The new missionaries were Americans financed by suburban congregations of a broadly Pentecostal persuasion. They created their own self-reliant networks of river communication and became largely independent of the state. The new missions, along with some old Catholic and Baptist ones, became one of the lasting legacies of the colonial order.

The colonial system of Portuguese Africa evolved a pragmatic compromise between racial segregation and racial assimilation. Before 1910, under the Portuguese monarchy, a significant number of black subjects had been given posts of influence and responsibility in the colonies because there were insufficient white immigrants to run the bureaucracy, command the militia, and staff the trading houses. A Creole community blended African customs with the lifestyle of the colonizer. After the establishment of the republic in 1910, an influx of white functionaries came to the colonies to seek the fortunes that had eluded them in Europe and drive black and brown Creoles out of their work stations. Discriminatory practices were not racially enforced as they were in Belgian or British Africa, however, and assimilated Africans could gain status if they were literate, wore European clothing, spoke metropolitan Portuguese, practiced Catholic worship, and demonstrated to an inspectorate of morals that they were loyal to the "mother country" in Europe. Angola's mixed-race population, whose fathers were white and whose mothers were black, was painfully caught up in a pattern of racial legislation so complex that by the end of the colonial period a mere 2 percent of Angolans had achieved assimilated status. Even the *assimilados* who achieved equality before the law soon discovered that under the dictatorial system of Salazar's so-called fascism legal status did not give citizens, white or black, the automatic right to participate in politics. What assimilation did provide was exemption from the forced labor regime, which by 1960 conscripted 175,000 of Angola's one million able-bodied men to work each year for colonial enterprises owned by whites. *Contratados* (compulsory recruits) worked for twelve months at a stretch for a minimal wage that did not allow them to contribute adequately to the living expenses of their dependents. The system provided a powerful downward pressure on wages since men "volunteered" for work at very low pay rather than risk being captured as forced labor. Forced labor practices drove as many as a quarter of a million Angolans to flee across the borders, where work for meager salaries in British, French, and Belgian Africa was preferable to conscription in Angola. Those who sought to evade rural labor raids without going abroad tried to find jobs in the cities, but influx controls similar to those used in South Africa authorized the police to raid the city slums and return rural peoples to their villages, ready to be seized by recruiting agents. Expulsion from the city not only discouraged the growth of a black urban proletariat but kept opportunities open for illiterate white migrants from Portugal. In Angola merchants, artisans, and truck drivers were predominantly white and filled niches held by Indians or Syrians in East or West Africa. Many working-class whites were so poor that they lived in multiracial slums and worked as market gardeners and street vendors. The old-established African fishing industry saw successful white hawkers take over the marketing of fish and later invest in new boats and new nets, which competed with traditional fishing methods. Angola's petty merchants created a class different from any found in Belgian or British colonies. A decline in African skills in the private commercial sector was matched by a decline in skills in the public sector. Whereas the Congo *évolués* were staffing government agencies and post offices by the 1950s, in Angola the reverse was happening: white immigrants were replacing black counter clerks and bookkeepers at the lowest levels. When independence came to Angola, there was a chronic shortage of personnel not only to maintain the commercial economy but also to staff essential administrative services.

One of the distinctive features of late colonialism in the Portuguese territories was the proud belief by the rulers that they had developed a lusotropical social class that blended African roots with Portuguese culture. The concept of lusotropicalism, imported from the mixed-race societies of Brazil, was used to justify the continuance of foreign overrule after the 1960 wave of decolonization in tropical Africa and to deny the charges of racism that critics directed at the Portuguese. The propaganda campaign failed, and in their social and racial composition Portuguese colonies came to resemble South Africa rather more than the new postcolonial societies of French and British Africa. Attempts to present the African colonies as overseas provinces of Portugal, equal in constitutional law to the domestic provinces, were economically and politically fraudulent. The racial prejudices introduced to Angola in the early twentieth century intensified during the 1950s, especially when white women began to arrive in larger numbers and dismissed the black concubines who had customarily provided settlers with marriage partners. The new colonial women also turned their wrath on the illegitimate offspring of casual unions, and no amount of government propaganda proclaiming that blacks were equal to whites in Portugal's harmonious empire could overcome the reality of an intense institutional racism. It was this racism that made the outbreak of the Angolan revolution in 1961 so violent and caused the shedding of so much blood on the streets of Luanda.

6

Race and Class in a "Fascist" Colony

The term "fascist" has been much misused by historians, and it is not at all clear that the term can appropriately be employed in relation to even the most authoritarian of the imperial powers. Although Salazar adopted some "corporatist" ideas from Mussolini, Portugal's dictator never swayed a mass movement in the way that Hitler could. Portuguese authoritarianism did, however, bite deeply and cruelly into the lives of African subjects, just as fascism bit deeply into the lives of many European peoples; Polish conscript laborers of the early 1940s in Europe might have been well placed to comprehend the agonies that Angola's forced migrants suffered when dragged off to the mines and plantations of Africa. This essay was written in 2004 as a preface to the forthcoming published version of Christine Messiant's 1983 doctoral dissertation.[1] Messiant's work examines and explains the deep background to the Angolan revolution of 1961, providing a key foundation on which new generations of Angolan scholars can build a fresh understanding of their society, their culture, and their history. It remains a pioneering study in grasping the complexity, diversity, and tenacity of the social identities that molded private and public behavior in Angola.

Angola has its own very specific amalgam of social forces derived from Portugal's Atlantic empire as well as from Central Africa's deep past. Several centuries of cultural, religious, and genetic blending created a social nucleus around the twin cities of Luanda and Benguela. In the Angolan interior, distinctive creolized communities grew up in Mbanza Kongo, Ambaka, and Caconda. The Creole enclaves enjoyed some international contacts and might bear comparison with colonized societies of the Americas, or with the British and Dutch in Asia. These societies were created during the centuries of the slave trade and modified by the advent of twentieth-century white immigrants. The new colonialism opened up an ideological debate as to whether black and brown subjects should be incorporated—assimilated—into colonial society and encouraged to acquire European skills and customs, or whether Africans should merely be hewers of wood and drawers of water. The spin doctors of imperial propaganda dwelt on the liberalism of assimilation and on the virtues of Angolans who had acquired civic status. The economic managers of empire, meanwhile, preferred to perfect a system of compulsory labor service that would underpin public and private enterprise and generate colonial revenue. In 1961 the violent strain of coercion caused the system to collapse in bloodshed. Colonial managers, migrant workers, and assimilated elites were all victims of a wave of killings that spread across Angola.

A shortage of whites had forced the early colonial state in Angola to conscript "social mestiços," wives and mixed-race sons, into the administrative class. The pragmatic incorporation of nonwhites into the colonial nucleus continued into the twentieth century despite the ferocious denunciation of miscegenation by the republican high commissioner, Norton de Matos. The gender imbalance continued after the 1926 creation of the "fascist" New State, and as late as 1950 Angola still had little more than half as many white women as white men. Whether the new generations of mixed-race children would enhance cultural loyalty to Portugal or would sow the seeds of disaffection and nationalism was a question anxiously debated among colonizers. One peculiarity was the status of mixed-race families descended from the 2,000 white convicts from Portugal who had lived in Angola in 1900 but were not listed in the colonial census. The tide of convicts continued to rise until the outbreak of the Second World War and may have accounted for 20 percent of Angola's immigrants. By that time another distinctive white community, the 2,000 Boer settlers in the south, had returned to South Africa. Proposals to replace them with Jewish settlers from Russia or white settlers from Algeria came to naught.

In attracting settlers to Angola, the key policy of colonization concerned land ownership. The colony had prospected unsuccessfully for petroleum after the First World War and had granted a mining concession that made diamonds the leading export until the Second World War. Settler wealth, however, derived from the alienation of fertile pockets of African farmland. Ninety percent of Angola's land was either uncultivated or unsuitable for cultivation. When whites took possession of three million hectares, they gained a mere 2 percent of the country's total land surface but 20 percent of good soils. The white seizure of land drove African producers onto less productive soils, where the colonial state compelled them to grow cotton and other revenue crops for white merchants. Increased pressure on poor soils did nothing to enhance land fertilization, and the cycle of fallow seasons traditionally allowed for soil regeneration grew shorter. The new, white landowners used the fertile, well-watered soils to grow coffee and other profitable export crops. The politics of land alienation were to haunt Angola throughout the twentieth century and remain the country's most controversial political issue in the twenty-first century. By then it was the African urban elite, including the generals of the two armies who had fought the civil wars, who aspired to become plantation owners. They wished to return to the agricultural agenda of the old white settlers and restore Angola's black peasants to their colonial-type status as farm laborers.

Portugal's interwar dictatorship aspired to create a colonial system sufficiently robust to survive the Great Depression of the

1930s. Portugal had been thrown into crisis by the closing of the doors to Brazilian emigration and the abrupt ending of South American wage remittances. Under Salazar the colonial office was pressed to generate alternative imperial revenues for the impoverished Iberian homeland. The policy, however much the fascists pretended otherwise, depended on allowing foreign capital to stimulate economic activity. The dictator minimized the cost of administering the colony by cutting all forms of social expenditure and allowing private investors to operate unfettered by moral or legal constraint. The new empire even restricted the old republican aspirations of white settlers in the civil service by coopting ill-paid but "assimilated" nonwhites into the bureaucracy. Assimilation in Angola was related partly to whiteness of ancestry and partly to association with long-established urban families. Access to the assimilated urban nucleus was not easy to achieve. One road to acceptance was through Protestant schooling, a process that distinguished newly acculturated Angolans from the traditional Catholic families. Despite the windows of opportunity for a few assimilados, the colonial tradition expected whites to be managers and blacks to supply labor. Attempts by international agencies to investigate Angola's labor practices were strongly resisted. Before joining the United Nations in 1955, Portugal declared that Angola was an "overseas territory," a province of Portugal, and not a colony at all. The attempt to avoid world scrutiny, as the French did in their Algerian départements, did not succeed, and the International Labour Organization resolutely condemned labor conditions in Angola during the years leading up to the coffee and cotton rebellions of 1961.

In 1960, 90 percent of Angola's sparse population lived in rural areas, on plantations, around scattered farmsteads, and in small villages. Only the other 10 percent lived in sixteen officially designated colonial towns. Of these townsmen a quarter of a million lived in provincial cities such as New Lisbon and Benguela or in remote administrative posts with civic status and architecture. The other quarter of a million urban Angolans lived in the city of Luanda. The late colonial population of Angola consisted of two million black adults, two million children, and a rising tide of white immigrants. Initially new immigrants came from unlettered peasant communities in northern Portugal and Madeira. When wives and children are included, total immigration rose to around 200,000 people, a figure comparable to the settler population of Southern Rhodesia and twice that of the expatriate population in Belgium's Congo. Most new immigrants chose to settle in towns and deemed themselves superior to the old "bush" settlers who ran small trading posts in the provinces. The number included several thousand educated, though often nonwhite, immigrants from Portugal's tropical islands. Management in both the private and public sectors came to be dominated by whites or by a few "colored" Cape Verdeans. Poor immigrants took up petty trading, and some African market women in Luanda were driven from their established street stalls by white rivals. Angola, unlike Mozambique, welcomed unskilled migrants. Their aspirations, however, caused distress, which was the background to the great nationalist awakening that virulently shook Angola's people in 1961.

The pain of white colonization was felt particularly harshly by conscripted black workers in the countryside. Conscripts were legally bound over to plantation employers for a whole year at a time, or, if they were posted to desert-coast fishing banks and frontier diamond mines, for eighteen months. Such schedules made it impossible for migrant workers to return home for seasonal planting and harvesting. Even the compulsory six-month home furlough to which migrants were entitled between contracts was not always observed. Although some laborers were recruited to work in their home districts, their daily shifts were so long that tending their own crops was well-nigh impossible. Abolishing "idleness, indolence, and vagrancy" was the watchword of the provincial governors who administered the cruel activities of the labor catchers. In 1946 Henrique Galvão, a colonial inspector who later became a prominent Portuguese politician, thought that the recruitment system was "in some respects worse than slavery." Ten years later Basil Davidson suspected that conditions had continued to deteriorate.[2] Only in 1959 was an official attempt made to enhance the wages of conscripts. A norm of 200 escudos a month was suggested, but this represented only about 2 British shillings a day (28 U.S. cents) at a time when laborers on the colonial Gold Coast had already negotiated 6 shillings a day. Even this tiny norm was not enforced, and white farmers continued to deduct more than half a conscript's wages for medicine, shelter, transport, work clothes, food, and other real or imaginary payments in kind. In effect wages remained at around 70 escudos a month (9 U.S. cents a day) for migrants and less for those conscripted to work in their own locality. At the end of each year matters were made worse when the colonial state tried to collect income tax, a tax which, incidentally, was rarely spent on building schools or clinics for native peoples.

The lack of educational facilities was particularly notable in Angola. Even neglected "Cinderella" colonies like Northern Rhodesia and Mozambique spent more on educating their black children, and Southern Rhodesia provided education for most of its black infants when only 5 percent of "indigenous" children attended school in Angola. When access to the modern world through education was denied, Angolans turned to modern religion, and communities of Protestants in the north and Catholics in the south grew in scope. In a country as fragmented, exploited, and deprived of labor unions and cultural organizations as Angola, missions, although not heralds of the revolution, became the unexpected focus of protest movements.

The net income derived from compulsory labor by Angola's uneducated rural masses was so meager that enterprising Angolans who had been registered as indígenas (natives) tried to find freelance contracts with employers of their own choice. Proof of such service could in theory be used to fend off the demands of recruiters seeking migrant labor. Farm work was never lucrative, and the better-paid alternative to local laboring or plantation migrancy was a job in town. In the northern town of Uíge wages could be twice the notional legal wage and in Luanda three times as much. Family dependents in town could further support the household by shining shoes or selling lottery tickets. Men with skills as nurses or artisans might upgrade their wages to 2,000 escudos a month during the urban boom, though barely 3 percent of common black folk made it to the city. In the north, east, and south of the country the best survival strategy was emigration. In neighboring countries French, Belgian, and British wages were higher, and even in Namibia a pair of boots cost a quarter what it cost in Angola. Some 100,000 of Angola's economic migrants worked for the 6,000 white Portuguese who lived in the Belgian Congo. Altogether, probably half a million Angolans lived abroad during the 1950s, and on the southern plateau it was said that everyone had heard of the fabled gold mines of Johannesburg.

Inside Angola class and race relations remained complex, and teasing out the various strands of non-native society has been one of Christine Messiant's most rewarding contributions to Angolan studies. Mixed-race assimilados were more numerous than black assimilados in schools, colleges, and seminaries, and they rose to higher ranks of responsibility in the church or the provincial administration. The highest flyers, in medicine and the law for instance, were commonly not Angola-born but were nonwhites from Portuguese India or São Tomé. Even locally born mestiços gained advantages over black assimilados and found it easier to obtain good jobs and to prove their status when rounded up in police raids. Mestiço children were not so obviously ostracized by white classmates as were black children who entered secondary school. Racism grew in the 1950s, however, and mestiço children tended to be considered the "children of blacks" rather than recognized as the "sons of whites." The number of excluded mixed-race children brought up as "native" by their unsupported mothers began to increase both in the towns and in the provinces, where they received no recognized status.

The number of registered "coloured" inhabitants in Angola, to use a South African term, never exceeded 1 or 2 percent of the population, as compared to 10 percent in South Africa. Despite its small numbers, Angola's mixed-race population had played a significant colonial role in the past. It had been distributed throughout the provincial towns at a ratio of one mestiço to every three whites, with notable clusters in Luanda, Benguela, Huambo, and Lubango. Mestiços were legally entitled to set up businesses and borrow capital. Their commercial activities spread from owning bars in the black townships of Luanda to trading in the coffee plantations of the north and the maize fields of the south. Most mestiços remained modest salary earners in government service, but in the 1950s assimilated Angolans were ever more sternly excluded from semiprivileged positions by an authoritarian political system and by the influx of unskilled whites who competed to fill the social layer between privilege and poverty that mestiços had historically occupied. New immigrants instilled a sort of petty apartheid into Angola, where previously social manners rather than skin pigmentation had divided society. This radicalization of social discrimination drove "civilized" Angolans back into association with the "natives" from whom they had so painfully struggled to distinguish themselves by language, eating habits, and mental outlook.

The controversial role played by the assimilated population in the emergence of a "nationalist" leadership among Angolans makes Messiant's search for the factors that defined the rival strands of class and status important. She identifies three categories of assimilados. Coloured Angolans, unlike coloured people in South Africa, were usually descended not from two coloured parents but from a white father who provided status to his children and a nonwhite mother. In the Angolan census of 1950 (but not in those of 1940 or of 1960) several thousand assimilados were enumerated as "white." The second category, "civilized" Angolans, mostly black but some coloured, belonged to the old high-status, Roman Catholic colonial nucleus, with ten generations of urban history behind it. The children and grandchildren of this ancient category of "aristocratic" assimilados provided one of the strands of the ruling elite that governed Angola during the civil wars of the later twentieth century. The third segment of assimilated colonial society emerged among the "native" population in the provinces. With mission support they gained sufficient education to win entry into society and sometimes, as in the case of the medical doctor Agostinho Neto, into the professions. After independence these old social categories inherited from a colonial age were challenged by new Angolan elites whose advancement was achieved through the army and the universities.

The history of Angola's cultural mestiços focuses initially on their real estate in downtown Luanda. When challenged by the 1910 wave of republican immigrants, many assimilados moved into marginal townships but retained their bureaucratic employment in the city. Their cultural association, the Liga Nacional Africana, continued to organize society balls and cultural lectures. A few were persecuted, or even sent into exile, where they established contact with assimilados living in the provinces. They mounted campaigns of protest over the erosion of the rights of nonwhites, but when the nationalist confrontation of 1961 broke out most adult assimilados preferred to lie low and protect such social advantages as they had managed to retain. Their children, however, were sometimes tempted to throw in their lot with the campaign for independence and join a hundred colonial students in Portuguese universities who abandoned their studies and fled to western Europe. The young radicals who abandoned their haughty historic families joined members of the new assimilated group, the children of artisans, catechists, traders, teachers, nurses, and office workers who had acquired modest status if not wealth. The new assimilados spoke Portuguese at work but not at home and did not belong to the same social clubs as the old assimilados. Instead they lived cheek-by-jowl with neighbors who had retained up-country contacts and African legacies. In politics, though old assimilados claimed the authenticity of history, it was the new assimilados who could most clearly hear the voice of the people. Both old and new came to recognize that after 1961 Portuguese colonialism, unlike British or French, was digging in for the long term.

The dream of colonizers in Angola had always been to find easy wealth in mineral extraction. In the sixteenth century silver had been the mythical lure, and a century later Salvador de Sà fought to conquer the small northern copper mines. In the eigh-

teenth century the marquis of Pombal built an iron foundry, which
he named Nova Oeiras after his Lisbon country seat and staffed
with Basque foundry men, but it had no lasting success. After 1926
minerals brought significant rather than merely symbolic change
to Angola. British engineers and financiers finally completed the
building of a railway from the Benguela harbor at Lobito to the
great Congo-Zambian copper mines of the Anglo-Belgian borderlands. The copper-carrying railway stimulated several ancil-
lary branches of colonial production. Huge eucalyptus forests were
planted, for instance, to fuel the locomotives with firewood. Down
on the desert coast a fishing industry expanded to almost half a
million tonnes a year, enabling it to export dried fish to the mining cities at the head of the line of rail. Highland peasants who
were not marched to the coast to gut and dry fish and were not
needed to clear the shrubs on either side of the railway were compelled to grow maize as a tax crop, their soils being too cold for
compulsory cotton. New canteens were opened at the railway sid-
ings by petty traders from Portugal. A railway required more than
the produce of farmers and fishermen to fill the trucks with pay-
loads. It also required personnel to repair the track, shovel the
ash, operate the signals, sell the tickets, and staff the telegraph
machines. Many of the necessary African railway personnel had
been trained in the Congregationalist missions that the Swiss,
Canadians, and others had set up in the highland kingdoms. The
uniformed staff on the Benguela railway were part of an old-boy
network that transcended the ethnic rivalries between the Ovimbundu kingdoms. Cooperation among a modernizing elite of petty
functionaries replaced historic antagonism and became one of the
bases of a political party created in the middle 1960s.

Angola was partially insulated from the ideological debates
that led to the postwar transformation of Africa. Britain, France,
and Belgium decided over the course of the 1950s to establish self-
governing regimes in the African colonies. A new black bourgeoisie that had been trained in the administrative practices of
the colonizers would take over responsibility for local politics. In
the matter of commerce it would work with the European powers

(and to a lesser extent with the United States and the Soviet Union) in a neocolonial association. Each postcolonial partnership would ensure economic and military stability in fragmented republics, helping the flow of wealth from the third world in the south to the first world in the north to continue uninterrupted. The neocolonial transformation of Africa in 1960 presented Portugal with particular problems. The black bourgeoisie in Angola was relatively small, and many of its middle-class leaders lived in semi-exile as social-democratic students in Lisbon or free-marketeering businessmen in Kinshasa. Those in Lisbon aspired to employment in the service industries of the state as doctors, teachers, agronomists, or civil servants. Some colonial students maintained covert links with white Communists who aspired to transform conservative Portugal into a radical socialist society. The socialism of Angolan students, however, was linked to a Protestant Christianity that many had acquired in the Methodist schools of Luanda. The exiles in Kinshasa had different experiences and aspirations. Their ethos was a capitalist one; they did not seek entry into state service or employment alongside colonial bureaucrats but aspired to replace white Portuguese immigrants in Angola's commercial sector. Their solidarity as a group was not only employment oriented but also ideologically based on a common religious culture derived from their schooling in the Baptist missions of both Angola and colonial Congo. The contrasted traditions of upwardly mobile middle-class exiles led to the creation of two rival political parties that were to compete with each other, as well as with the Portuguese, in the forthcoming struggle for independence.

The idea of black self-government caused acute anxiety to the colonial settlers in Angola and the imperial regime in Lisbon. The government's fears were increased by the sudden and unexpected loss of Portugal's tiny but historically prestigious colony in India. The settlers' fears were increased by the disorder that accompanied the transfer of power in Congo. Rumors of black noncommissioned officers refusing to obey their white superiors and of frightened white nuns being jostled on the street by exuberant black crowds caused unease in Angola. Congolese were observed to expect that independence would lead to an immediate transfer of wealth and status from white to black, and exaggerated rumors of conflict and disorder were relayed into Angola. As a result, all signs of Angolan insubordination were met with excessive repression, panicking both white and black communities. Early in 1961 the Portuguese government flew its tiny air force to Africa to bomb the villages of starving cotton farmers, while settlers in the city armed themselves with knives, cudgels, and even firearms to kill town Africans who enjoyed enough education to threaten the expatriate hold on white-collar jobs. The greatest colonial explosion of 1961 occurred in Angola's coffee belt. Coffee pickers paraded relatively peacefully up to a farmhouse to ask for arrears of unpaid wages. Their gesture was seen as a threat to white prestige and imperial authority and the demonstration was fired upon. Revolution immediately broke out as white expatriates killed black functionaries, dispossessed local farmers killed foreign estate owners, and day laborers killed contract migrants. The bloodshed exceeded anything that the British had witnessed on their coffee estates in Kenya during the Mau Mau war. The quasi-fascist empire armed settlers as instant vigilantes and then conscripted an expeditionary force in Europe to restore colonial authority. Almost one hundred thousand north Angolans fled across the border into Congo, where they remained for the last thirteen years of the colonial era.

The aftermath of the revolution of 1961 was dramatic and unexpected. Far from bringing a transfer of power from colonial officials to African politicians, it brought a new phase of active colonization with new foreign investment, new white immigration, and new education and training. The development of radical innovation in what had been thought of as a moribund Portuguese dictatorship was surprising. Portugal skillfully blackmailed President Kennedy into supplying American weapons to repress the rebellion. The extractive economic nationalism was replaced by an investment climate that created a manufacturing sector. Portuguese entrepreneurs in Angola expected to replace the Belgians in Central

Africa and export textiles, plastics, household goods, cement, and beer to Congo. Portuguese army officers, modeling themselves on the French in Algeria and the Afrikaners in South Africa, found new status, prestige, and wealth. Profits made from war were invested in high-rise buildings in Lisbon. The coffee industry flourished with rewarding prices in the new European Community. Oil wells opened by American technology generated royalties that transformed Luanda into a thriving city. The old-style British colonial businesses were partially replaced by new Portuguese financiers and technocrats from industrial families supporting Salazar's New State in its great leap forward.

The economic boom that lifted Angola in the early 1960s had several important consequences. The first was the arrival of large contingents of willing rather than reluctant white migrants, who came as expatriates seeking wages in the cities, not as settlers seeking a permanent future in the colonies. They came to escape from the mournful culture of fado songs and Catholic pilgrimages to enjoy the open climate of palm trees, motor scooters, and beat music in a socially emancipated Africa. The rising young colonials were not the only ones who benefited from the economic revival. Some Africans gained skills and escaped from poverty, forced labor, compulsory planting, and rural indebtedness. The muddy, diseased, and dangerous black slums of Luanda had schools, jobs, and wages that were a magnet to rural migrants. Black migrants to the towns lived cheek by jowl with illiterate whites who had begun their colonial careers as hawkers and chambermaids before gaining status positions as stall holders and supervisors. White and black both competed for city jobs with the mixed-race children of the 1950s. On the frontiers of the white asphalt suburbs and the marshy black slums the distinguished assimilado families hovered on the social borders of white, black, and brown communities. It was in these twilight communities that modern politics began to take root.

The revolution of 1961 caught the exiled politicians of Angola by surprise. In Kinshasa exiles, seeing themselves as the true nationalists who deserved to inherit power in an independent republic of Angola, scrambled to take credit for the challenge to colonial power that the coffee rebellion represented. They gained international support from some of the political factions in Congo and also from the United States and China, both of which valued their strongly anti-Soviet ideology at a time when the Soviet Union was apparently gaining ground in Africa. Their attempt to enroll new refugees into guerrilla regiments that could roll back the Portuguese army and claim northern Angola as their own was not a great success. Northern guerrillas occasionally made life in the coffee belt dangerous and forced some planters to build security fences round their estates, but the politicians remained in exile until 1974, when a colonial ceasefire enabled them to move into Angola. Some settled in the coffee belt, where a new class of black capitalists supported by peasant cooperatives had emerged during the last colonial years. Returnees with financial and merchant skills aspired to replace fleeing white storekeepers and artisans. The great magnet, however, was the city of Luanda. Although northerners failed to capture the city politically, they did so economically and built up a flourishing informal sector whose enormous markets fed and clothed Luanda.

The rivals to the northern capitalists from Kinshasa were the bureaucratic socialists from the student clubs in colonial Lisbon. They called themselves the Popular Movement for the Liberation of Angola (MPLA), and it was they who captured the government of Luanda in 1974. Their long march back to the city from whence they had originally come was more traumatic than that of their rivals across the Congo border. When war broke out in 1961 they had had difficulty in finding a haven of exile in which to set up a government-in-waiting. In Brazzaville they trained a guerrilla force to penetrate the forest of Cabinda but did not seriously dent the security of the colony. In Zambia they were handicapped by their hosts' dependence on the Benguela railway, which they were not permitted to disrupt with guerrilla sabotage. In Tanzania their seaport headquarters was two thousand kilometers from home along very unreliable roads. Frustration led to factionalism, rivalry, and despondency, resulting in the withdrawal of support by the Soviet Union. In addition to being harried by Portuguese security forces and their black scouts, the MPLA freedom fighters were challenged by a third political movement that sprang up in southern Angola in the mid-1960s. Neither this southern movement nor the northern movement that it gradually eclipsed, nor indeed the MPLA itself, was in command of events when the Portuguese empire collapsed. The transformation of Angola in 1974 took all exiled politicians by surprise just as the revolution of 1961 had done.

By the beginning of 1974 Angola had reached military, political, and economic stalemate. Militarily there was little movement. The war of liberation had already acquired undertones of civil war as the Portuguese made secret agreements with rival guerrilla factions to encourage them to fight each other. Politically the country was run by unelected officials appointed by Lisbon, and very little consultation took place even with the white population, let alone the black one. Economically the boom years had come to an end as debts mounted and the coffee revenues did not keep pace with either consumer expectation or government expenditure. The oil industry was not yet controlled by its producers, as it was to be after the OPEC initiatives of 1973 and 1979, and Angola could not anticipate the huge mineral royalties that it was later to gain. A significant factor in the recession was the financial disappointment of the officer corps in the colonial army, which could no longer envisage long-term benefits for itself in Africa. Army officers began to consider the option of colonial withdrawal. At the same time Portuguese industry began to measure the potential benefits of joining the European Community, especially since Europe had attracted twice as many Portuguese migrants as the empire had done. The benefits of holding Angola by force involved levels of military taxation that industry resented. In April army captains mounted a coup, to which the captains of industry acquiesced. In Lisbon they established a series of provisional postfascist governments that explored the road to decolonization.

Angolan decolonization brought many unexpected twists and turns. Most settlers and expatriates initially assumed that little economic change would occur and that their administrative and technical expertise would guarantee them continued employment. When civil conflict between black political rivals broke out, whites continued to assume that "native restlessness" would not affect them any more than the colonial war in the bush had done. When shooting matches moved into the cities, however, settler optimism gave way to anxiety and, fifteen months after the colonial cease-fire, a sudden panic seized Angola's white population. Ninety percent of the Portuguese in Angola abruptly left the country, packing all the colonial wealth they could carry into wooden crates. Black servants gained some pickings from the stampede, but much property was wantonly destroyed. Three parties emerged from the three guerrilla armies. The northern party turned to Congo and borrowed its military regiments in an unsuccessful attempt to capture Luanda. The southern party turned to South Africa in an equally unsuccessful attempt to capture Luanda with a flying column of white commandos. The MPLA, which took some time to settle its internal differences, turned to Cuba for help, and Cuban troops flew to Africa to hold Luanda with weapons bought from Yugoslavia. Portugal decided to abandon Angola to the "people" rather than to any one political party. The three armies of intervention pounded each other around the perimeter of the capital as the last Portuguese governor slipped away on a dark-ened gunboat. Fourteen days later, on November 25, 1975, Portugal's own revolution was terminated by a second military coup d'état. The new government showed little interest in Angola's affairs, and civil wars accompanied by foreign interventions continued to break out. The colonial legacy, however, continued to grow, and Angola retained Portugal's heritage of language and literature, of gastronomy and culture.

7

The Death Throes of Empire

This first part of this chapter was written in 1980 as the world was trying to come to terms with the complex nature of Angolan politics and the unexpected violence of the aftermath of empire. At the time, and for some years afterwards, the international print and broadcasting media had a simplistic tendency to assume that if the violence was in Africa, the cause must surely be tribal. This painless form of analysis was taken up by diplomats and politicians. Even the great Nigerian civil war was readily explained in terms of tribalism, without any attempt to explore the deeper concepts of modernization, acculturation, education, conversion, commercialization, and professional and personal ambition in civilian and military life. Such issues later became familiar to Angola watchers. The last section of the chapter was written in 2004 and draws attention to the new source material and new scholarship of the last 25 years, which have shed fresh light on the death throes of the Portuguese empire.

The normal explanation for Angola's fractured nationalist movement and subsequent civil wars is that they arise from ethnic divisions rooted in a thousand years of incompatible linguistic, cultural, and political evolution. This "tribal" explanation, much favored by the media at the time, can be called into question. Did not the politics of confrontation arise out of rival traditions of urban modernization rather than from the old rural base? Should not the solidarity of the Europeanized leadership be attributed to old-school networks? There is a need to investigate how far Angola's three civil war armies instilled regional patriotism through the use of Protestant—Congregationalist, Baptist, and Methodist—church hierarchies and church hymns. Was the march to war caused by modernizing forces even shallower in their time depth than the hundred-year-old Protestant churches? In the last colonial quarter century business interests proliferated, and it cannot be entirely coincidence that the two major African nations to undergo severe postcolonial civil wars, Nigeria and Angola, both did so at a moment when oil prospecting was at the point of reaching significant production. Alternative explanations can also be sought in international strategy, in the tensions of the cold war, in the western protection of South African investments, in the frustrations of Cuban revolutionary failure in the New World. Each level of investigation presents the historian with difficult tasks in approaching the sources. Within Angola political mobilization occurred not only in church congregations but in cultural associations and football clubs. Military success depended on arms shipments from Soviet satellites, financial backing from Texan oil companies, and combat training by experts in South Africa, China, and Algeria. Mercenaries came from as far away as Bradford in England. But always the trail leads to the scrambled files that the CIA tried to protect from America's Freedom of Information Act. The United States, in 1975, was seeking enemies in Africa.

On Monday, April 7, 1975, the night sky in the city of Luanda was illuminated by gunfire. Earlier that day there had been rumblings in one of the black shantytowns. Jeeploads of four-party patrols had swiftly quelled the confrontation, but not before some bloodshed had occurred. The night shooting appeared to involve heavy weapons, and the target—intended or accidental—was a South African passenger jet flying low over the northern suburbs.

Only minor damage was caused to the plane, and after refueling it returned to Johannesburg. A Portuguese aircraft, allegedly carrying the country's future president, later landed unhindered.

The bullets in the fuselage of a South African plane represented a turning point in the history of southern decolonization in Africa. But were they the last shots of an old war or the first shots of a new one? Was this the culminating achievement of armed black nationalism, which had gained power in Katanga and independence in Mozambique and was now about to decolonize Angola? Or did those shots relate to the militant return of white power and a failed attempt to assassinate the future leader? The questions raised by the events of April 7 all require historical explanation, but there is much disagreement over the historical depth that it is necessary to plumb. To the average journalist the cause was "tribal": ethnic antipathy, rooted in deep tradition, impeded the growth of a national purpose and set people against people with "inevitable savagery." Nothing else was expected of "barbarous" Africa and therefore no effort was required to explain the incidents of the day as they edged Angola closer to civil war. The country's uncomfortable complexity and rapid social change were ignored. Instead the country was rationalized into three static "tribes" for the benefit of world newspaper readers.

The concept of tribalism in Africa cannot, however, easily be justified as the long-term growth of a common cultural consciousness. Small village societies were commonly more important in popular awareness than later ethnic ones. Precolonial cohesion was not a marked trait even among peoples speaking a common language. The political unity of northern Angola, which had been so striking in the sixteenth century, had given way to intense warlord rivalries in the eighteenth century. The interaction of theology and commerce, of politics and family, that had once strengthened the institutions of the old Kongo kingdom had turned to undermining and destroying them. By the nineteenth century no observer saw northern Angola as being peopled by a single Kongo tribe. The historian must therefore seek alternative roots for the common political purpose motivating the northern armed movement that took part in the events of 1975. The presumption of an ancient Kongo ethnic solidarity cannot hold.

The argument in favor of historic unity in the two other broad language zones of Angola is even less compelling. The great highland populations of the south never achieved any political cohesion in precolonial times. A dozen trading kingdoms competed sharply for control of markets, caravan routes, ferry crossings, iron mines, clay pits, farmland, and the Atlantic trading harbors. Cooperation was based on fierce commercial bargaining, armed military deterrence, and royal marriage alliances, not on a common Ovimbundu national purpose. Such a purpose had emerged only in the face of external threat and the intensification of colonial penetration in the terminal phase of empire.

The third media-inspired "tribal nation" was said to be descended from the late-medieval kingdom of Ndongo, whose king, the Ngola, gave Angola its name. This kingdom had been overwhelmed three centuries ago by European conquest, and any "traditional" ethnicity in Angola's middle zone had been overlaid by social groups that had responded to new colonial opportunity to create Luso-African Creole communities. The hybrid culture of Portugal and Africa influenced diplomacy and international relations far into the interior of Africa. A literate class of soldiers, clerks, and commercial agents, known as the Ambaquistas, became the representatives of Portuguese enterprise and the precursors of empire. The proto-imperial social culture did not foster a Kimbundu ethnic solidarity; to the contrary, it divided society into collaborators and resisters, laborers and labor recruiters. Colonial conquest scattered the Kimbundu into pockets of isolated refugees in forest fastnesses where fighters held out against the unifying force of colonial conquest.

If ethnic loyalties and tribal animosities cannot be seen as the basis of war, a different alternative should be found to explain the rift in Angolan society that led to the shootings of April 1975. This alternative may be the division of the colonial presence in Angola. In most colonies in Africa the modern sector of society, and its attendant educational and employment opportunities, were

based in a single colonial capital. Angola was different. Throughout the twentieth century it had three focal points. One was indeed the capital, the Portuguese city of Luanda. Another, across
the northern border, was the Belgian city of Kinshasa, known for
some decades as Léopoldville. The third was the southern port of
Lobito. This division, it might be contended, was far more fundamental socially and economically than the old vernacular frontier that separated the hinterland of the three cities. Emerging
twentieth-century politics revolved around leaders whose identities were formed in the modern sector of society. Traditional
leaders, with a few exceptions, had limited importance in this polarized late-colonial society. In Luanda government bureaucracy
was the traditional black first step on the ladder of economic opportunity. This opportunity was always fragile and could be threatened by the spasmodic immigration of poor whites from rural
Portugal, who gained preference over black migrants from rural
Africa. Skill, literacy, and experience counted for less than color,
and competition over urban employment fostered a black political leadership in Luanda in the 1950s. Competition led to conflict
and an outburst of city warfare in February 1961. Those black
town dwellers who escaped into exile formed a new generation of
leaders and created a quasi-Marxist political party, the MPLA.

The second city to which Angolans looked for opportunity was
Kinshasa. It was a city of refuge and of exile as well as of education and employment. Those who went there learned French as
their passport to status and achievement. It might be argued that
literacy and a difference of modern language among city dwellers
were more significant in politics and in war than a difference of
vernacular and popular speech. The Kinshasa Angolans found
work in small African and expatriate business firms more readily
than in the Belgian bureaucracy. Their early history, however,
was overlaid by the huge influx of 100,000 refugees that swept
into Congo in 1961. The new escapees tried to get to the city to
find employment, or in a few cases to join the incipient armed
groups that exiled political leaders tried to mobilize. These Kinshasa leaders remained quite distinct from those whose cultural

roots were in the rival city of Luanda. Their party became the FNLA.

The third city to which rural Angolans drifted, or were compulsorily drafted by forced labor practices, was the southern port of Lobito. An even newer town than Belgian Kinshasa, it began to replace the old roadstead of Benguela in the 1930s after the great Copper Belt railway was finally completed. Any explanation of the divisions of Angolan society needs to examine the rise of the dockworkers of Lobito. The old port of Benguela had been founded in 1615, and its *mestiço* bourgeoisie identified fairly easily with the politicians of Luanda. The brash new city of Lobito had no such cultural roots, and its population of highland immigrants proved a fertile recruiting ground for a third political party, UNITA, whose leaders lived along the line of rail. To attribute the distinctiveness of UNITA to ethnicity before seriously attempting any urban social history would seem premature.

Angola became a nominally Catholic country during the course of the Portuguese conquest, which gained momentum from 1875. The Catholic Church was not, however, a mission church with a mandate to proselytize, heal, and educate. It was a branch of the metropolitan church and therefore primarily concerned with the white expatriate and settler community and with the assimilated elite of black and mixed-race peoples who associated with them in commercial and administrative centers. Only in the far south did a Catholic mission church of French and Alsatian parentage make a predominant impact. In the rest of the country the colonial regime left a partial educational, spiritual, and medical vacuum that Protestants sought to fill. The three Protestant churches that took root in the rural areas of Angola before 1961 provided features that affected the distinctiveness of the three political parties that grew up after 1961.

The Baptist Church had chosen the north as its field of activity in the 1870s. From the outset its activity, although missionaries did their utmost to avoid conflict with the civil authority and to instill concepts of law and order among their converts, was seen as a threat by Portugal. Despite their caution Baptists were seen by Africans as a safeguard against commercial or government exploitation. In 1913 the northern faith in Baptist benevolence was so strong that when rebellion broke out in villages from which men were being seized and taken to the logging forests of Cabinda, the colonial administration felt sure that the Baptists had fomented revolution. The British mission minister, the Reverend Bowskill, was arrested and accused of seditiously undermining the loyalty of Portugal's colonial subjects. For the next half century, until the revolution of 1961, relations between mission stations, village deacons, and the colonial state remained tense. During the thirteen-year colonial war after 1961, although officially Portugal had declared all northerners to be Catholic, African loyalty to the Baptist Church surreptitiously grew. A Baptist underground movement became the symbol of resistance. Toward the end of the war the dragooning policies that repressed Protestants gave way to a political campaign for hearts and minds, with a tacit recognition that negotiations would succeed only if conducted through recognized Baptist elders. The colonial army, though not the settlers, even recognized that economic liberalization would reduce the revolutionary nationalist temperature, and so soldiers facilitated the creation of farmers' cooperatives approved by the church.

In central Angola the Methodist Church, complete with its American-style bishops, served a similar role to that of the northern Baptists. It created an integrated leadership of high school graduates, lay preachers, and medical orderlies that was not under official supervision even in the capital. The social columns of the mission newspapers provide an unrivaled insight into the kinship web of modern colonial society in the twentieth century. By the late 1950s this structure became linked to initial attempts at mobilizing embryonic political movements. One question that arises is why it was Methodist families who were most prone to adopt Marxist ideals when contemplating a liberation struggle. Methodists, unlike Baptists, were predominantly urban and were often employed in bureaucratic positions by the state. A planned economic order offered them better prospects than a free-market one.

They could idealize peasants, but their own economic interests related to salaried service rather than to commercial production. Baptists in the rich coffee zones, by contrast, held tightly to capitalist concepts of land ownership and the hiring of wage labor. Out of Methodist aspirations a black preacher's son rose to become a Marxist president.

The Congregationalists, whose churches emerged among the Ovimbundu people, were even more successful than Methodists or Baptists in facilitating the mobilization of a mass party, though the process started much later on their high plateau. Television footage from 1975 shows huge rallies singing political hymns to Presbyterian tunes. The suddenness with which UNITA mobilized highland peoples into a new common loyalty was surprising. Their leaders were the first to achieve a ceasefire agreement with the Portuguese, and cooperation began even before the Lisbon revolution of 1974. In Jonas Savimbi UNITA had the most charismatic of the political leaders. The highlands had not suffered the long history of military failure and recriminatory schisms that had so bitterly affected the rival parties farther north. Southerners, threatened by land hunger, land alienation, and labor conscription, developed a tradition of hostility both to city government in Luanda and to city entrepreneurs from Kinshasa. For a short while the UNITA leadership even studied Mao's theories of rural politicization.

Studying the social impact of semiclandestine churches in a warring colony involves more than understanding the ambitions of farmers and office workers. The role of business activity in Angola's politics became increasingly significant during the colonial war. In 1963 Portugal liberalized its financial policy of self-reliance and allowed new foreign investment to generate new forms of wealth with which to wage the war of colonial reconquest. When the Lisbon revolution of 1974 overthrew the "fascist" rulers of empire, Portugal abruptly turned away from Africa and toward Europe. International business interests in Angola had to reassess their position. In 1975 the world suddenly became convinced that Angola possessed hidden riches. In the style of the original scramble for Africa, foreigners began to safeguard their resources for fear of rival claimants. They gave political levies, mineral royalties, and voluntary contributions to political movements and guerrilla armies. The FNLA, for instance, was given funds to buy Luanda's leading newspaper, published in the heart of its opponents' MPLA territory. The financial links between Angola's exiled politicians and the personal copper fortune of President Mobutu of Congo may never be unraveled. Meanwhile, the biggest of Angola's oil companies, Cabinda Gulf, decided to gamble both ways on the outcome of the decolonization conflict and to match U.S. funding for the FNLA with comparable royalty funding for the MPLA. African gunrunners such as those that Frederick Forsythe portrayed in *The Dogs of War* may already have been active in Angola, as they had previously been in Nigeria, and may have supplied the weapons used in the aircraft incident of April 1975. But whoever did supply those weapons, it seems likely that the partisans shot the wrong plane.

Thirty years after the shooting episode of 1975, one of the legacies of the past that most blights the lives of twenty-first-century Angolans is the range of discrepancies in wealth and status. These discrepancies make harmonious nation building particularly arduous. Women, for instance, who bore so much of the burden of African economic survival throughout the second half of the twentieth century, are largely excluded from real power in modern society in much the same way that they were marginalized in both colonial and liberation politics. In the same way village communities are excluded from the respect and status offered to affluent city gentlemen, whether in suits or in uniforms, much as they were excluded in the 1960s. The power of education is also used, and abused, in a country where few ordinary children are given even the rudiments of schooling while the children of the ruling families obtain international diplomas in prestigious foreign boarding schools. In Angola the life of a worker is seen as cheap in the eyes of a manager; while one drinks river water bought from a truck, the other drinks Evian water, which costs nearly as much as whiskey. All these discrepancies cry out for explanation, and a good social history of Angola's people during their long years of struggle is needed by all—by politicians, by social and medical workers, by schoolmistresses, by business managers, by university students, by the international white Land Rover brigades. The Brazilian scholar Marcelo Bittencourt has provided some basic tools with which to make such studies and modestly hopes that his work on contemporary history may stimulate others to publish new memoirs, letters, poems, plays that will stimulate the imagination of Angola's people and shed light on the half-remembered past, the death throes of empire, with which all of them will have to come to terms.[1]

Many of the attempts to understand Angola's history in the second half of the twentieth century have been undertaken by foreign scholars, who, while deeply sympathetic to Angola's protracted traumas, come from another world and often write in another language. The initial work depended very much on political analysis, on diplomatic documents, on interviews with leaders of the many factions and fractions that made up the nationalist kaleidoscope. Gradually, however, the voice of the voiceless began to be heard through such dramatic initiatives as the Jaime and Barber interviews.[2] Hard on their heels comes the Bittencourt volume, which digests and integrates the works of the international scholars, highlights and expands the range of the interview material, and, most strikingly of all, makes the first extended use of the archives of the Portuguese political police, the secret and much-feared PIDE. The police records enable serious scholars to get a better grasp than before on the factionalism that marked Angola's political history in that era.

The study of factionalism in the Angolan liberation struggles follows cycles of fashion, at one moment emphasizing ideology; at another, ethnicity; at another, foreign sponsorship; at another, educational culture. Always the skills, ambitions, and weaknesses of individual militants, politicians, diplomats, and entrepreneurs play a role. So too do the minor irritants or comforts of life on the move, in exile, in rudimentary camps, in rented mud huts. Who has food, cigarettes, the right to steal a kiss from a pretty girl, a smart new uniform, or an old-boy friendship with a party treasurer? And always race is part of the colonial mind-set, so prevalent that foot soldiers making little progress on the ground wonder if Agostinho Neto or Daniel Chipenda, both of whom have white spouses, might not have made a secret deal with the "tribe" of his in-laws. Being even half white in Angola may lead to accusations of petty bourgeois snobbery and neglect of the welfare of the two or three thousand men in the MPLA's various miniregiments of guerrillas.

Bittencourt's convincing understanding of the interaction between daily life and liberation politics is based on his admirable range of new source materials, including his own interviews conducted on visits to Luanda between 1995 and 2000. The timing of the interviews is felicitous since the founding fathers—Angola has very few founding mothers—now are elderly or have died. Those who survived were often able to respond to long and detailed interviews that sought to clarify, from various vantage points, the new questions that archival papers have raised. But writing the history of a guerrilla war presents several severe challenges. The first of these is the frequent absence of documents written during the decision-making meetings held on the ground. Political movements that formed, splintered, and re-formed in cities of exile or rudimentary forest camps did not have the resources to keep many archival papers. The very creation of the MPLA is subject to rival memories and interpretations. As Christine Messiant has said with humorous perspicacity, "Amongst ourselves even the past is unpredictable." But some documentary fossils do turn up in unexpected places, such as American university libraries, where some dispassionate scholars have been able to make good use of them. Bittencourt, however, has been able to make excellent use of an unexpected set of archival treasures: the propaganda papers, and even some of the internal policy documents, that Portugal's secret police captured from nationalist sources. Ironic though it may seem, the defeated colonizing enemy preserved a better set of records than the victorious liberation movements. The documents frozen in PIDE files have not undergone

the process of adaptation that oral records undergo as each sur-
vivor tries to interpret his or her personal trajectory in the light
of rapidly changing circumstances.

The records of the political police, which began its activities in
Angola in 1957, contain a second type of information that is much
more difficult to interpret than captured papers: the transcripts
of interviews conducted with Angolan people who had been seized
by military and police action. In assessing these highly tenden-
tious data Bittencourt has the advantage of a Brazilian background
with a historic memory of the effects of government-orchestrated
terrorism on the people of Brazil from the mid-1960s to the late
1970s. As Umberto Eco graphically tells us in *The Name of the
Rose*, the use of torture to obtain information can have dramatically distorting effects on the data extracted from the screaming
victim. Further distortions occur when prisoners of war reinvent
their own positions and roles in order to gain advantage out of
unintentional misfortune or treasonable aspiration. It is to Bittencourt's credit that his book is fully sensitive to the care that
must be taken in using police reports. In Angola torture was used
not only in dark cells to extract information, but also in open
displays of army terrorism as village leaders were publicly de-
capitated to dissuade colonial subjects from even thinking about
independence.

Some of Bittencourt's best insights weigh the factors that so
deeply marked Angola's political activists in the months of transition before and after the fall of Portugal's dictatorship on April
25, 1974. In these years lassitude and disenchantment overcame
optimism and ambition after ten years of ineffectual struggle.
Blame and counterblame, leadership bids and counterbids, solidarity and fragmentation, class rivalry and ethnic fraternity all affected
both the FNLA and the MPLA and even the then-minuscule
UNITA, with its 300 isolated militants covertly attempting to
make military alliances with Portuguese troops in the deep highland interior. The rumblings, accusations, arrests, and executions
that accompanied the slow evolution and later rapid dissipation of
the eastern revolt are lucidly laid out. The debates, subversions,

and plottings of the intellectuals of Congo-Brazzaville, who became the Active Revolt in May 1974, are also explained in convincing terms. Beneath both of these tendencies, and the abortive leadership bids of Daniel Chipenda and Joachim de Pinto Andrade, lies an interesting discussion of the readjustment movement, which came from China and affected both northern and eastern wings of the MPLA. Throughout Angola's independence struggle China was a distant, little-known force with unpredictable effects on the nationalist scene. One of Angola's founding fathers, Viriato da Cruz, retired from active politics to settle in China, and both the MPLA and FNLA, at varying times and to varying degrees, were dependent on the assistance that China gave both to the socialist republic of Tanzania, where Neto had his headquarters, and to the capitalist dictatorship of Zaire, which sheltered Roberto's home base. In the early 1970s, however, it was the Chinese fashion for self-criticism that took hold in the Angolan camps of both Congo-Brazzaville and Zambia. Open seminars attended by large numbers of middle cadres and common foot soldiers discussed the predicaments of exile, the wisdom and failings of the leadership, and the injustices and inequalities that separated the "civilized" guerrillas (from Angola's towns) from the "indigenous" guerrillas (from the countryside). None of the leaders was comfortable with Chinese-style open debate or grassroots criticism, and in interviews in the 1990s both Lúcio Lara, from the Congo front, and Daniel Chipenda, from the Zambia front, remembered the unease they had felt. Agostinho Neto was even more bitter in his condemnation of any dissidence, but as absolute ruler of his movement he controlled the money and was able to move back and forth using stick and carrot to punish disloyalty and reward the faithful—a style of political management still much in evidence in present-day Angola.

The importance of Bittencourt's book is in the light it sheds on experiences that Angola's people have to understand and absorb as they seek their way toward modernity and social justice. Both the colonial and the anticolonial experiences were sometimes cruel and autocratic, riddled with prejudice and inequality.

Current struggles to create a climate of open debate in Angola, with a vibrant civil society and a choice of political directions, are hampered by the weight of a past that needs to be sympathetically understood. It is encouraging that a brave Brazilian has given excellent signposts toward that sympathy and understanding.

8

Destabilizing the Neighborhood

The 1980s were a peculiarly distressing time for the peoples of Central Africa, including Angola. Wars of destabilization, partly orchestrated by the superpowers, broke out between South Africa and its neighbors. This chapter is a modification of the penultimate chapter of Frontline Nationalism in Angola and Mozambique, *a small book written at the request of Unesco and published in 1992.*[1]

Nation building would have presented quite enough difficulties in Angola and its sister colony of Mozambique if the new generation of black leaders had been left to attend to their task unhindered by outside influence. Instead, outside powers became increasingly involved in forcing their choices and undermining their actions. The oldest foreign influence in the region (apart from colonial Portugal itself) was the Republic of South Africa, which had long cast its shadow over its northern neighbors. When the two new lusophone nations gained independence, they almost immediately accentuated their ideological and economic differences with South Africa by assisting the struggles for independence in Zimbabwe and Namibia. Spasmodic South African interference in the affairs of its neighbors gradually became a systematic policy of destabilization. Intervention increased after the fall of John Vorster when the army became the key political actor inside South Africa. Foreign hostility to Angola and Mozambique brought together an unholy alliance of enemies from the Congo River to the Cape of Good Hope. The forces of destabilization were recruited among black exiles as well as white settlers, among commandos from the former colonial armies, and among disappointed politicians from the nationalist movements. South Africa's policy brought damaging foreign intervention from outside Africa. Superpower involvement in Mozambique was predominantly covert, but in Angola a war by proxy between the United States and the Soviet Union replaced Vietnam as a focal point of cold war confrontation. The victims were now African rather than Asian, and they were deliberately hindered from building proud, independent nations with the freedom to choose their own development strategies.

During the old colonial war South African military intervention in the affairs of its neighbors had been limited. Some military equipment of American origin was sold or leased to the Portuguese at nominal prices. Counterinsurgency experts made strategic recommendations on guerrilla warfare, though Portugal was too proud to accept South African advice readily. South African assassination experts might have had a hand in making the parcel bomb that killed Eduardo Mondlane, the first president of the Front for the Liberation of Mozambique (Frelimo), though internal conflicts within the movement may have created the opportunity. South Africa was not above the use of murder, as demonstrated by the 1982 killing of Ruth First in her university office in Mozambique. It is symptomatic of the climate that when President Machel of Mozambique was killed in a plane crash in 1986, observers were predisposed to suspect foul play and blame the South African policy of intervention in Mozambique.

The military origins of intervention concerned the war of liberation in Rhodesia, which had escalated in 1972. When Mozambique won its independence two years later, it decided to support the freedom fighters in Rhodesia and help impose economic sanctions on the white regime of Ian Smith. When Mozambique, one of the poorest nations in the world, followed UN requests to suspend communications and transport services to the Rhodesians, it immediately became a victim of Smith's economic reprisals. The political cost of imposing sanctions on Rhodesia was even higher than the economic loss of earnings. Mozambique provided a haven for refugees escaping from the Rhodesian war and offered training grounds for soldiers going into the war. This black solidarity with black Zimbabweans brought commando reprisals by white Rhodesians and air raids by white South Africans. By 1979, however, South Africa, fearing that any prolongation of the Rhodesian war might spill over its own border, brought the antagonists to the negotiating table, and a cease-fire opened the way for a black government to rule Zimbabwe. The government that Zimbabweans elected was not quite as pliant as South Africa had expected, and Pretoria began plotting further military interventions in the frontline states.

In 1978 a sea change had taken place in the politics of South Africa. The long-serving prime minister, John Vorster, had based his effective strategies of black repression on the work of the police force and the intelligence services. A cowed home front had enabled him, despite the fact that the doctrine of apartheid prevailed at home, to reach out and build bridges with tropical Africa in countries where South African goods could be sold. This strategy came under threat when Mozambique and Angola moved toward more radical regional policies than those of South Africa's pragmatic partners in Malawi or Zambia or Congo. Radical liberation movements beyond the border led to the growth of a black consciousness movement that revived the hopes of South Africans. Demonstrators began to boycott segregated buses, and a trade union movement even attempted strikes despite the threat of reprisals. Most dramatically, in 1976 the children of Soweto rose in rebellion after years of quiescence by their parents and challenged apartheid with unbowed courage. The Mozambican slogan, *a luta continua* (the struggle continues), was proclaimed with clenched-fist salutes by black South Africans.

The white South African response to the black revival was to dump Vorster as prime minister and appoint an army man in his place. P. W. Botha gradually brought the army to the center of South African life. Soldiers were increasingly used to maintain so-called law and order and soldiers were invited to sit on sensitive political committees. Above all—from the point of view of Africa's nationalists—soldiers now intervened forcefully in foreign policy. The policies of détente and dialogue were systematically replaced by policies of confrontation and destabilization. Botha wished to eliminate the external wing of the African National Congress while at the same time suggesting to the world that nationalists such as the black rulers of Mozambique were incapable of governing themselves responsibly. His regime's antinationalist propaganda made effective use of the Soviet presence in Angola to portray the South African army as the defender of "civilized values" against the spreading threat of communism. A forward foreign policy won the army an increased share of the budget, provided its officers with more rapid promotion, permitted modernization of weapons systems, and gave soldiers power at home. An old guard of white industrialists protested quietly at the rapid rise in taxation that the militarization of South African politics entailed and regretted the loss of export markets in independent Africa. Such protests were not strong enough to override the army's preferred policies, not even when civilian politicians were ready to negotiate compromises with black nationalists in Mozambique or Angola.

The South African army's decision to destabilize Mozambique proved to be distressingly easy. First, they sought out disaffected Mozambican leaders whose ambitions had not been satisfied in the nationalist framework. Secondly, they recruited and supplied with guns white Rhodesian commandos who had fled south at the independence of Zimbabwe. These Rhodesians were experienced in fostering terror not only in Zimbabwe but also during cross-border operations inside Mozambique. A third line of support came from Portuguese settlers who had fled to South Africa or Portugal and sought to re-create the colonial El Dorado they had lost. Mozambique's antinationalist coalition sought sympathizers among black exiles in America and mounted an effective public relations campaign in Washington to persuade both the U.S. government and black American opinion that it was a legitimate political force rather than a front for South African military operations. Finally, Frelimo's opponents, the Mozambique National Resistance (Renamo), approached the new generation of British neocolonial tycoons that was being groomed to move into Africa in the Thatcher era. The Lonrho Corporation, whose head had been described by a previous Conservative prime minister as representing "the unacceptable face of capitalism," now became the accepted vanguard of the new British capitalism in Africa. Businessmen waited for the time to be ripe for Mozambique to abandon its idealistic radical notions and turn to the West for help in rebuilding an old colonial economy that had provided cheap sugar, cotton, and rice for industrialists in the world's rich north. Fighting a war on two fronts, against poverty at home and enemies abroad, proved too much for Mozambique, which had neither the economic resources nor the managerial talent to take on another long war.

In 1984 President Machel asked for peace and met President Botha on the banks of the Inkomati River. The accords they signed should have reassured South Africa that Mozambique would not be used as a base for attacks on South Africa by black exiles, and should have reassured Mozambique that South Africa would stop arming and transporting the Renamo guerrillas, who had by then made virtually the whole country ungovernable. The accords suited many of the parties to destabilization. They suited the South African government, which was bearing the cost of the attack. They suited international business, which was convinced that Mozambique was now ready to cooperate along the archtraditional economic lines laid down by the International Monetary Fund. They suited the European Community, which admitted Mozambique to the Lomé club of its tame third-world suppliers. They suited Britain, which was anxious to reopen the railway to Zimbabwe and accelerate the development of economic partnership with its former settler colony. But they did not suit the South African army, for which peace would involve retrenchment and redundancies, and they did not suit the Mozambique guerrilla leaders, who sought to replace the nationalists in government. The war therefore continued.

The second stage of the Mozambique war of destabilization was significantly different. It is true that for most of the rural people the insecurity was as terrifying as ever. Village women going to the stream for water were still liable to be captured by terrorists and taken away to serve as porters and provide sexual services for the soldiers. Young men were still press-ganged into the opposition's regiments of irregulars. Barnyards were still raided nightly for food. Refugees still streamed across the borders to Malawi and Zimbabwe, where they received a bleak welcome from host populations themselves suffering from drought, food shortages, and underemployment. But at the strategic level the terms of the war had changed. Britain no longer supported South Africa wholeheartedly in its Mozambique policy; now it offered the nationalists help in training a new officer corps for the Mozambique army in exchange for economic access to the country. Even more dramatically, Zimbabwe sent 10,000 troops into Mozambique to protect the railway from South African attack. International business even began to estimate the cost of rebuilding the hundreds of electricity pylons that had been destroyed by commandos to prevent the use of the great Cabora Bassa power supply for regional development and integration. By the end of the 1980s the new climate seemed to be in the ascendant. Peace seemed possible by the time South African politicians drove President Botha out of office in September 1989. Meanwhile the international focus of destabilization had shifted to the long-running war in Angola.

Mozambique had won its independence as a result of military victory and embarked on nation building with some degree of euphoria before the realities of poverty and the enmity of its industrial neighbors soured the celebrations. In Angola independence was gained by compromise after the confrontation of three intervening armies that tried to replace the colonial forces. The population of the capital city may have felt a spasm of euphoria when the guns were held at bay, though not beyond earshot, throughout independence day on November 11, 1975. The rest of the country had little to celebrate under the weight of Zairean and South African occupation. Gradually, however, in the months after independence the forces from the capital regained authority over the provinces. It was therefore with some surprise that the victorious nationalist party, the MPLA, discovered that the first challenge to its rule came from its very own base in Luanda city.

After the war of intervention, frustration rose rapidly among the urban poor to reach a revolutionary peak in 1977, two years after the transfer of power. Political cells had grown up in the mushrooming shantytowns of Luanda. Former employees of colonists who had fled now scraped along below the bread line. The withdrawal of industrial capital had led to the closure of manufacturing plants and the creation of serious unemployment. Insecurity in the countryside and the vision of a city paved with gold led to an uncontrolled influx from the rural areas. MPLA party cells began mobilizing the underprivileged quarters of the city and establishing discussion groups that drank in the revolutionary dogmas of Mao and Enver Hoxha. Radical ideologues emerged from both the guerrilla movement and its expatriate camp followers. The mobilization of the underprivileged took place under the guise of organizing football clubs and other innocuous activities, but the head of the black radicals, Nito Alves, was a member of the central committee of the MPLA. On May 27, 1977, he attempted to mount a coup d'état but was foiled, captured, and shot along with his closest associates. The episode cast a clear light, however, on the difficulties that the nationalists faced in creating an independent stable nation in Angola.

The attempted coup of May 1977 came as a surprise to many observers, though the evidence subsequently published shows that it should not have. Confrontation had been building up within the central committee of the MPLA since the previous October, yet it was not in the capital that the MPLA expected to experience difficulties. In this respect the politics of Angola after the Portuguese cease-fire were markedly different from those of Mozambique. In Mozambique Frelimo was a rural-based movement that faced its greatest initial problems in accommodating to the entrenched economic systems of the industrial cities, where expectations were at variance with those of long-standing party recruits from the north. It was therefore not surprising that Mozambique experienced patches of turbulence in the capital during the transition of power. In Angola, by contrast, the MPLA did have city experience in Luanda, Benguela, and Malange, and its difficulties, highlighted by the war of intervention, were in accommodating to the rural populations of the north and the plateau. As the search for accommodation went on, the attempted coup illustrated how deeply the stresses of the war had bitten into the MPLA's urban constituency, which it had previously taken for granted.

If the first challenge to the power of the MPLA nationalists came from their own backyard in Luanda, the second came from a much broader front in the provinces. The heroes of the revolution had been the workers and the peasants. The workers in the capital had discovered that their expectations had been pitched too high and independence was not all golden. The peasants learned the same lesson even more bitterly. They had been painfully incorporated into the market economy by the colonial power in the 1960s. Now in the 1970s and 1980s they were even more painfully torn away from market opportunities. By the 1980s peasants in almost all areas of the country were disenchanted with their government and open to the suggestion that alternative political movements might offer them a better range of opportunities. The short-lived rebellion of the town was followed by the long-lasting rebellion of the countryside.

Three factors made the rural rebellion in postindependence Angola particularly tenacious. First, it suited the South African government to follow up the civil war, within a very few years, with a war of destabilization comparable to the one that it was conducting in Mozambique. Secondly, it suited the United States not to recognize the MPLA government, which had eluded its control and, still worse, had sought help from the most sensitive of America's opponents, the Cubans. Thirdly, the provincial rebellion had a political focus that began with highland political mobilization by UNITA and continued with the militarization of UNITA in the far lands of southeastern Angola, where troops could be protected by South African air cover. The result was a new war with fierce international involvement.

The Angolan war gained in intensity during the 1980s and in the process tore the Ovimbundu highlands apart. By 1990 it was estimated by Africa Watch, the human rights organization, that thousands of people had been captured by UNITA guerrillas from the highlands and taken to the south to create an internal colony. The Ovimbundu, who represented some 40 percent of the total Angolan population, found themselves attacked by both the forces of UNITA and the people's army of the MPLA government.

The objective of UNITA was to impoverish zones under government control by indiscriminate robbing, killing, and burning. Survivors who failed to flee were then marched to the "liberated zones" beyond the reach of government forces. Women were taken as well as men, and children were especially prized as future guerrilla recruits. To hinder normal economic development further, plow oxen were stolen and seed grain eaten. Worse still, the farm paths were strewn with hidden land mines so that peasants attempting to return to their fields risked being maimed or killed. The UNITA policy of bringing the government to its knees by starving the peasants caused the death of half a million children in the 1980s. Malnutrition in the towns to which the people fled was accentuated by ambushes on the convoys that tried to supply them by road. Even medical convoys were ambushed without mercy. Nearly two million vulnerable people were further weakened by drought at the end of the decade.

The atrocities of war were not confined to antigovernment action. On the contrary, the MPLA strategy of confining UNITA to the southeast and preventing it from returning to the highlands as an effective political force involved equal hostility towards the highland villages. To prevent the insurgents from developing a social base, the government determined, by removing the people who might sustain enemy operations, to "drain the sea" in which guerrillas might swim like fish. The MPLA government, assuming all free peasants to be potential UNITA sympathizers, adopted the same arbitrary and inhumane strategy as its colonial forebears and herded people into barbed-wire villages under armed guard to deny them any possibility of contact with opposition forces. The moving of hundreds of thousands of farmers from their familiar terrain intensified the shortfall in food production in the 1980s. Even the soldiers often went hungry and had to loot food convoys. Young men who tried to evade conscription were subject to violent reprisals. Village leaders suspected of disloyalty to their harsh government were detained by officials of the Ministry of State Security.

Many highland peoples tacitly surmised that a change of government would bring an end to the hardships, and UNITA remained surprisingly popular. But as the situation deteriorated, the war spread to other provinces and the leadership of UNITA became increasingly authoritarian. Jonas Savimbi had once been a charismatic leader with grassroots support and foreign admirers. Some of his lieutenants were men from the business world with a foreign education and international connections. As the war dragged on, however, interpersonal violence increased, and a once-sympathetic biographer of Savimbi began to recognize the scale of the torture and killing that went on inside the guerrilla organization.[2] In the "land at the end of the earth," the politics of semi-exiles in the 1980s were as brutal as had been the international strife of the 1970s, when it was the MPLA that tore itself apart on the remote margins of Angola.

Although the MPLA gained relatively firm command of the city in the 1980s, it was eventually forced by the ongoing war in the provinces to change its ideology and government practice. With gentle encouragement from Cuba, attempts were made to seek a policy of harmonization and economic reform. The scale of corruption and inefficiency was such that even the huge oil revenues could not compensate for the decline into austerity. Before any internal political reforms could reach the top of the national agenda, however, the foreign war with South Africa had to be resolved.

The war of destabilization in Angola was no less devastating than the one in Mozambique, though it was very different in kind and in effect. A nationalist government in Angola was less of a military threat to South Africa than one in Mozambique, whose capital lay only a few miles from the Transvaal border. Ideologically, however, radical nationalism in Angola was potentially inflaming to black opinion in South Africa and thus, according to white thinking, needed to be curbed. A campaign of destabilization was therefore undertaken in Angola. Although the war of the 1980s was in some respects similar to that of the 1970s, the balance between the "civil" and the "intervention" elements had altered. In the 1970s the fractions of the nationalist movement were still powerful enough to compete with each other for central authority. In the early 1980s the domestic opposition forces had largely withered, confined to the UNITA enclave and its highland sympathizers, but the foreign presence had grown stronger. Regional opposition strategy, orchestrated by South Africa, and intercontinental opposition strategy, orchestrated by the United States, dominated the Angolan war of the 1980s.

The first international change to affect Angola was the defeat of President Carter in the U.S. election of 1980 and his replacement by Ronald Reagan. Carter had restricted the level of U.S. involvement in local superpower confrontations and reduced the support that the United States afforded to South African strategic planners. Reagan came to power determined to stem the third-world search for national autonomy. His regime armed and financed client groups in what were euphemistically called "low-intensity conflicts." Although of low intensity by the standards of the Pentagon, they were devastating in their toll on human life and their disruption of social and economic development.

In Angola the chosen vehicle for the low-intensity campaign to arrest nationalist aspirations was the old liberation movement, which had failed to gain power in the civil war. UNITA, the former client of China, was rebuilt, rearmed, and given a protected military base as the new client of America. This base was far outside the movement's old political constituency, but it benefited from a powerful South African air shield administered in the nearby Caprivi territory of Namibia. While South Africa protected the rebel movement, the United States orchestrated a propaganda campaign to challenge the legitimacy of the government. Collaborating with South Africa caused some embarrassment to the U.S. administration, but the alliance nevertheless survived throughout the 1980s, partly because the West wanted to protect Namibian uranium supplies for its nuclear energy industries and was anxious to deter Angola from providing a haven to Namibian freedom fighters. When oil prices dropped and nuclear energy began to appear ecologically risky, the need to hold Namibia weakened, but by then South Africa was committed to destabilizing Angola for geopolitical reasons.

The South African invasions of Angola in the 1980s had a rather different effect on world opinion from those of the 1970s, when moral revulsion at seeing the armies of apartheid marching into independent Africa brought some sympathy to the struggling government of Angola. In the 1980s South Africa was able to manage its public relations better. The Angolan government was now supported by a Cuban expeditionary force of 30,000 or more troops, which South Africa represented to the anxious West as "Moscow's Gurkhas." South Africa's attempts to destabilize a potential Soviet satellite in Africa attracted political support from Europe and financial support from the Middle East. By 1988, however, South Africa began to feel that the military and political cost of trying to overthrow the Angolan government outweighed the prospective gain. Sophisticated Soviet technological resistance supported an ever more experienced Angolan army until a cease-fire could be negotiated with the encouragement of a new U.S. president, George Bush Senior. Although the war had scarcely interrupted the flow of Angolan oil to Texas, the United States was ready to explore new economic opportunities in Africa and no longer deemed it necessary to challenge the disintegrating Soviet Union or preserve the colonial status of Namibia. Namibia gained its independence; South Africa deposed the old crocodile, President Botha, and readied itself for democracy; Mozambique achieved peace at the second attempt; but Angola continued to reap the whirlwind.

9

Carnival at Luanda

The Luanda carnival is the modern incarnation of street celebra-
tions that have been a central part of the life of the city since the
seventeenth century. In independent Angola the carnival has lost
its association with the Catholic calendar, but it has retained po-
litical dimensions that date back to imperial days. A more im-
portant feature of the carnival than either politics or religion is its
social dimension. The carnival represents a rivalry between the
various communities of the city that takes the form of competitive
dancing. The carnival becomes an exuberant display of wealth
and ostentation as the fishing families dress their daughters in
gorgeous costumes in which to dance to the rhythm of the drums.
But this chapter also suggests that the carnival represents, and al-
ways has represented, the pride of the common folk as they vigor-
ously deny their powerlessness before the western-suited brokers of
city politics. An earlier version of this essay was included in a
festschrift dedicated to Roland Oliver that appeared in 1988 in
the Journal of African History *and is reproduced here with the*
kind permission of the publisher, Cambridge University Press. A
Portuguese version of this account appeared in 1991 in the jour-
nal Análise Social.[1]

On Friday, March 27, 1987, Luanda celebrated its carnival on the magnificent palm-fringed boulevard that sweeps along the bay past the pink Grecian dome of the Bank of Angola. The date was a political one, unrelated to the Lenten calendar, but the festival was deeply imbued with rich symbols of Angola's history. For four hundred years Luanda has been the premier city of Africa's Atlantic seaboard. The dynamic continuity of popular culture had been little ruffled by the coming and going of contrasted regimes—Spanish Hapsburgs in the 1580s, Protestant Netherlanders in the 1640s, Brazilian planters in the 1660s, Portuguese mercantilists in the 1730s, black Creoles in the 1850s, army monarchists in the 1880s, white republicans in the 1910s, "fascist" authoritarians in the 1930s, industrializing capitalists in the 1960s, nationalist revolutionaries in the 1980s. The carnival and similar feast days have always represented a flexible response to the traumas of change, a tight hold on the values of the past, and an ironic portrayal of how to exorcise contemporary devils.

Popular acclaim for the Luanda carnival was as old as the city itself, though the occasion on which to celebrate had changed over the centuries. The choice of significant dates for public processions was as important to the political authorities of the past as it became to the party managers of 1987. In the seventeenth century the city fathers spent far more of their budget on feast days than on drainage or lighting. Attendance in full regalia at the great processions of state and church was compulsory. The choice of date for the 1987 carnival represented an attempt by the state, in its latest incarnation, to capture a popular base in Luanda. The Angolan state and its ruling MPLA party suffered, like most states and most ruling parties in Africa, from chronic weakness. The carnival therefore seemed to present an ideal forum in which to mobilize grassroots support. The constituency consisted of two hundred carnival groups located in all the numerous quarters, townships, parishes, shanties, fishing villages, asphalt suburbs, and high-rise slums of the metropolis. Each community had a sharply differentiated set of social attributes and reflected its identity in an ostentatious carnival image. The most successful groups appeared in the great procession, where thirty-three finalists competed for the prize and status of champion. The ruling political party decided in 1977 that the procession should henceforth be held on March 27, the date of the South African withdrawal from Angola after the "second war of liberation" in 1975–76. This date was chosen from among possible anniversaries with some care. May Day, in particular, was considered and rejected as being insufficiently linked to local political achievement. The expulsion of the South Africans was selected as the one unsullied patriotic achievement that might be grafted onto the growing charivari of a traditional carnival.

Breaking away from the Christian calendar and choosing a political date for the carnival was symbolically important. To revelers a four-day festival ending on what had once been Ash Wednesday was observed in full, and no government decree could restrict drinking time to a single bank holiday. For politicians the church was a potential threat to their state, and it was therefore important for the party to unravel even vestigial associations with organized religion and weave the threads of carnival into the fabric of civic loyalties. The Catholic Church, though weakened by proscription in the Portuguese revolutionary wars of the 1830s and by persecution under the imperial republic in the 1910s, remained the largest church in Angola and under a Marxist government was liable to become a focus of opposition as it had in Poland. In Angola the capture of a Catholic festival by the state was seen as a significant achievement, the creation of a civil religion, complete with borrowed ceremonials. Alongside the sponsorship of carnival, some MPLA party leaders maintained an uneasy relationship of adolescence with the Methodist Church in which they had been raised. More difficult was their relationship with the Ntoko Church, an independent black church influenced by the Kimbanguist Church of Congo. The growth of Ntokoism was seen as a disquieting challenge to the party's agenda for political education, and Ntokoists were treated as subversives, like Jehovah's

Witnesses, rather than as good patriots. In the weeks before the 1987 carnival one Ntokoist congregation came into armed confrontation with nationalist security forces and blood was shed on the road to Catete, a symbolic place of colonial martyrdom where MPLA heroes had once fallen to Portuguese security forces.

The 1987 carnival was divided between witnesses and actors. The interaction between the two was complex. On the central stand, flanked by the ministerial fleet of black Mercedes-Benz cars, the party hierarchy were witnesses. For them the carnival was the tenth Carnival of Victory, and the odd placard was hoisted before them portraying Botha-the-enemy or Kaunda-the-comrade. But at another level the hierarchy was much more intimately linked to the historical reality of the carnival as experienced by the participants. In origin, the carnival is emphatically the carnival of Luanda, and some members of the ruling party's political bureau had their cultural roots firmly embedded in the traditions of the city. They belonged to the historic Creole families that survived the social Darwinism of the early twentieth century, survived the mass influx of settlers at midcentury, survived the wilderness at the ends of the earth during the guerrilla war. They had now recovered the military tradition and past influence of their forebears to govern the army-led regime of the popular front. Some branches of the great congeries of Creole families dated back to the seventeenth century and had a long familiarity with carnival-type celebrations, though as members of the government they were detached from the popular participants.

The second covered stand of witnesses constituted the haute bourgeoisie of middle-class Luanda. In contrast to the old black Creole elite, many among the twentieth-century upper class were of recent mixed ancestry. Marrying light had commonly been the racial ambition of social climbers in Luanda, and the women and children seated under the civilian awning at carnival were a testimony to the continuity of custom. The first great influx of white immigrants to Angola consisted of republican carpetbaggers flocking to Africa in search of petty government employment

after the Portuguese revolution of 1910. On arrival they drove
the old Creole functionaries out of their bureaucratic positions
with loud racist cries of self-justification. Once settled, however,
they were often forced by circumstance to marry black wives and
thereafter give preferment to their own *mestiço* children. A second wave of immigrants came with the coffee boom of the 1950s.
Although this brought a significant influx of white females, some
male immigrants continued to marry black and even to make obei-
sance to African custom by adopting circumcision for themselves
and giving bridewealth to their in-laws. In the colonial generation having a white parent facilitated access to scarce education
and hence to employment and status. The educated mestiço population temporarily enhanced its prominence when in 1975 90 percent of expatriate whites left Angola. The mestiço class was no
match, however, for the Creole elite in the political struggles of
the 1980s, although mestiço wives and children of the administrative bureaucracy were given a covered stand at the carnival.

A third witness enclosure at the carnival contained the diplomatic corps, hot, bored, and overdressed. The only symbolism
that they recognized was the intrusion into the carnival of an
alien troupe of Afro-Caribbean dancers, jesters, drummers, and
harlequins sent from Cuba, Angola's Iberian Creole partner. The
diplomats were constantly on the qui vive for relative rise and decline in the pecking order of international friendships. Angolans,
by contrast, were not interested in mere foreigners. The Cuban
troupe did not even feature on the printed order of ceremony.
The populace had given the final cheers and begun to depart before the supposedly grand Cuban finale. After the intense symbolism of the home groups, the death masks and painted skele-
tons of the Cuban artistes were irrelevant to the huge crowds of
plebeian witnesses who had lined the streets for six hours without shade. Historically, however, carnival in Catholic America exceeded the parallel developments in Latin Africa, and the Cuban
link of 1987 mirrored the ties between Luanda's great festivals
and Brazilian ones.

The feast that can be most readily compared to the modern-day carnival is the canonization feast of St. Francis Xavier in 1620, which is fully described in Ralph Delgado's history of Angola.[2] The Jesuits of 1620, like the politicians of later times, wanted to harness customary celebrations to their own cause. They therefore contributed richly ornate floats to St. Francis's procession. They also included moral sketches such as the seven-headed monster that depicted pride as a lion, avarice as an ass, covetousness as a dog, libertinism as a sow, rage as a leopard, and gluttony as a wolf; sloth was somehow linked to Brazil. The governor, a conquistador from one of the great Jewish finance houses with slave-trading interests, ordered naval cannonades and night illuminations throughout the city. The army paraded and gave musket and arquebus salutes. The Luanda bards competed to write praise songs for the new saint. But for all the innovations and all the need of persons in authority to be seen in their most resplendent finery, the strength of the 1620 procession lay in its popular cultural roots.

Traditionally carnivals exorcise social ills and traumas through ridicule. The 1620 procession was led by three white giants (presumably puppets), far too large to have been comfortable in the cramped berth of a European sailing vessel. Dressed in formal wear, they were accompanied by their "father," a black dwarf captured in the Ndongo wars, who wore a velvet tunic of scarlet with white shoes and a rainbow beret. He railed at his huge white "children" with a thousand jokes and witticisms. To a country that had recently gone through the most devastating of all its slaving wars, the tableau must have had considerably more poignancy than trite ecclesiastical homilies about the seven deadly sins. But joking relationships were not enough to help a venerable but impotent old man overcome the striding might of the conquistadores.

The second group in the 1620 procession was a dance troupe sent by Creole society in São Tomé, the offshore island where slave-worked sugar plantations had been developed to a lucrative level of proficiency even before Columbus opened up the New

World. The troupe was led, like its twentieth-century counter-parts, by a puppet king whose prowess was acclaimed by accompanying praise singers. These were followed by sword dancers in the Portuguese style and by a ballet in which the daughters of the city worthies portrayed shepherdesses. The central float represented a Neptune-like god, the local saint of the sea folk of the Luanda shore, and the worker of miracles. The float, shaped realistically in the form of a whale, had an altar shrine on its back and was pulled by the king of the sea. Its tail was decorated with gold, shells, and silk braid. The lord of the waves, a deity lounging in a green, white, and red costume, was serenaded by an orchestra of four sirens. His dancing cortege sang ballads associated with fish, the mainstay of the shoreline economy.

Three further tableaux represented the condition of Africa in 1620. Angola, the colonial kingdom, was a figure dressed in green, with a blue turban quartered like a crown, a train of gem-encrusted gauze, and white boots covered in buttons and gold chain. Kongo, the Creole kingdom straddling the merchant world of the Atlantic and the terrestrial world of Africa, was similarly attired and brought gifts of rare price. Ethiopia, the land of the blacks, was dressed in the mode of the country, a simple loincloth around his waist, but he was the one who gave alms to the poor and scattered small silver coins, like Maundy groats, which the crowds caught rapturously like crowds catching beads at New Orleans carnival. The procession represented a syncretism of pagan rituals from the Mediterranean pantheon, of Christian rituals from the Iberian church, and of Mbundu and Kongo rituals designed to foster fertility and prosperity. Carnival was also an attempt to come to terms with the disasters of colonial conquest. The tradition carried on down the centuries, with constant modification, before being reenacted in the "Popular Republic" of independent Angola.

In the nineteenth century the colonial aspect of Luanda festivals was significantly modified. The Portuguese Revolution of 1820 to 1851, like the French Revolution that preceded it, was vigorously anticlerical. In 1834 the monastic houses were dissolved and their lands were sold to a new class of barons to ensure their support for the changes that revolution had wrought. In Angola one Luanda church, heralding a new scientific age, became a meteorological observatory. Meanwhile the monarchy passed into the hands of the ubiquitous house of Saxe-Coburg and the style of the Portuguese kings and queens came to resemble that of the bourgeois monarchies of Louis-Philippe and Victoria rather than the imperial grandeur of Louis Napoleon. The royal birthday became the official occasion for public ceremony and the competitive display of sartorial ostentation. For the 1846 birthday of King-Consort Ferdinand an effigy of the queen of Portugal was carried in a cortege through Luanda. Historical festivals continued to be celebrated under the bourgeois monarchy. Every August 15 the defeat of the Dutch by Salvador de Sà was a feast day, as indeed it would be until the fall of the last colonial government in 1975. Regattas also became part of the nineteenth-century festival scene: children paraded in striped uniforms while brass bands supplemented the traditional drum ensemble and the orchestras that used both African and Mediterranean stringed instruments. And despite all the innovations adopted at Luanda, religious festivals soon crept back.

In 1887 Héli Chatelain witnessed the Luanda carnival at a dinner attended by some of the stiffest members of Portugal's colonial bureaucracy. The gentlemen, preening themselves in cravats, went apoplectic when their wives suddenly abandoned all decorum, rose up from the feminine ranks of the oppressed, and put boot polish on the faces of their guests before showering them with bags of flour. The Presbyterian bachelor looked on with apparent good humor as the self-important world of the colonial elite was turned upside down. He also went out into the street to see how the black population of nineteenth-century Angola had made carnival its very own form of cultural expression and protest. The people of the street enthusiastically mocked the fearsome powers of their overlords.

The key scholarly document relating to the evolution of the Luanda carnival is the Parisian doctoral thesis of Rui Duarte de Carvalho, who, while studying the fisher folk of Luanda, witnessed the reincarnation of Luanda's traditional street ceremonial in the postcolonial victory carnival.[3] The Luanda carnival is rooted in the customs of the fishing communities but linked to the various levels of modern society. In 1987 each carnival group was governed by a *comandante* (commander), representing an office once feared and respected for both its military rank and its colonial authority. His headquarter was called the *quartel* (cantonment), a term likewise advisedly military by choice. The comandante was chosen for his skill alone and could be an immigrant or a peasant from the land rather than a true coast dweller, so long as his managerial skills warranted his appointment. The group also elected a president, who had to be a Luanda citizen, but "one of them" rather than "one of us." He wore a suit and tie, went into the "paved city," and talked to bureaucrats, administrators, and even politicians if the need arose. The president played no role in the dance but was related to the prestigious carnival sponsors. For its dance master the carnival group chose a king, who dressed up in the finest clothing his group could afford and wore a crown as in the procession of 1620. The king's consort was a resplendent queen who enthused the crowd and caught the eye of the judges. The royal couple were attended by the *conde* (count), who resembled the knave in a pack of cards, and by a princess. The king, the queen, and all the dancers were chosen for their talent rather than their social status. The lead singer, the standard bearer, and the bandmaster were normally married into an elite family. Charm carriers protected the drums from evil rivals, and straw torches were used to warm the drum skins. Gourd bearers supplied liquid refreshment to the musicians. The dancers were decked in vigorous colors, the wealthier teams being clothed in matching cotton prints. Each group symbolically demonstrated its profession, such as the fishermen by net throwing, while marshals kept the crowds back by vigorously mimicking police truncheon blows. The rear of the procession was brought up by jogging supporters, surging forward or dropping back as the dancers progressed.

The financing of the carnival groups was by public gift. The spectators put banknotes between the lips of the queen as she danced. The notes were then passed to the treasurer, who gave them to the nurse, who locked them in her bag. The military nursing sister as a key figure of dance societies is also found among the dance societies of German East Africa. Similar rituals of public fundraising can also be witnessed in the great parades of the Kimbanguist Church of Congo, where columns of dancing worshippers file past their leader depositing their contributions. Carnival revenue was used to regenerate the group and renew its costumes and musical instruments. It was also consumed, part of the income becoming the private revenue of the king, the queen, and the comandante, but some was put aside for mutual assistance and funeral funds.

Banners and emblems were carried in the carnival procession. One homemade placard bore that quintessential message of class warfare in Africa: *cuidade com o cão* (beware of the dog), a message seen as *mbwa mkali* on wrought iron gates in Nairobi, as *chien méchant* in Libreville, or in its Amharic version on the aristocratic portals of Addis Ababa. Guard dogs and the protection of property and privilege live on in the proletarian subconscious long after colonialism has died. Protests at continued social stratification were bravely displayed to the well-fed witnesses on the carnival tribune. More historic tableaux involved slave whipping, litter bearing, and other forms of remembered subservience and indignity. Independence had not yet alleviated the great stress felt as Angola went through the anguish of social transformation and periodic bouts of civil war.

The dance societies of the Luanda carnival resemble the *beni* dance societies of eastern Africa in ways that raise interesting questions.[4] How far is the mimicking of ceremonial sartorial styles based on antagonism and mockery and how far is it based on admiration and the aspiration to achieve European status? In colonial Lubumbashi the Belgian authorities saw dance societies as mocking colonial authority through satire and threatened dance troupes with arrest. In Malawi, by contrast, the clean orderliness of the dance societies was appreciated by the colonial administration, which saw no hostility to itself. In Luanda the carnival seems to have been officially encouraged during the 1950s, and there was even talk of dances being performed by colonial police sepoys. After the 1961 uprisings, however, carnival was banned, in a belated acknowledgment by colonial administrators of its potential for mocking the establishment and encouraging national aspiration.

A second comparative question concerns the importance of colonial consciousness in the dance societies. In eastern Africa the dance societies resolved tensions between former slaves and old-style freedmen, between coast-born Swahili and up-country peasants, between the "posh" and the "vulgar." In postcolonial Luanda rivalry between competing groups was more important than outward political messages. Carnival was highly localized, and preferred rivals were those adopting similar dance traditions and belonging to the same interlocking territories and families. Well-known neighborhood personalities were challenged with provocative songs that revealed moral weaknesses, private foibles, and social lapses. Allegations of incest and witchcraft in particular provided grist for the song mills of the Luanda bards. After each carnival it became necessary to lower the social temperature until a normal joking level of badinage had been restored.

One dance group that expected to become champions in the 1987 Luanda carnival was the Union of 54, a fisherman's union like some of those in the 1620 parade. The community from which it arose had lost its fishing bank in 1944 when unusual tides swept away the middle section of Luanda island. The families settled under the baobabs on a mainland beach and rebuilt their canoe fleet, made up of dugouts carved from the light trunks of *mafumeira* trees cut on the banks of the Bengo river. For centuries boatmen had earned a living by ferrying canoeloads of Bengo river water around the headland and into the bay to supply the city with salt-free domestic water. Real economic muscle, however, derived not from water carrying but from fishing. Seine nets, weighted with shells and buoyed with wooden floats, were drawn toward the beach, while larger prey had to be caught on lines equipped with expensive lead weights. Fishing has always been a man's task, and the heaviest work was done by migrant youths known as Bailundos, an ethnic label derived from the labor-exporting kingdom of Mbailundu, which lost control of its own highland destiny in the colonial war of 1902. The powerful master fishermen are Muxiluanda, and it is they who run the serious competitive business of commanding the *varina* style of carnival dance group.

The women of the fishing communities are responsible for fish marketing and sometimes wield as much power and influence as men. In the late colonial period, however, fishwives lost control of the wholesale trade to white European fishmongers who elbowed their way in with trucks. Women retained only the retailing side of the business until after independence, when they regained the initiative. A hierarchy of marketing evolved, with control in the hands of six dominant female entrepreneurs. Influential fishermen recognized the power of women in the community and chose their place of residence carefully to gain best matrimonial advantage. Both men and women sponsored carnival groups, but the money contributed by women determined the success or failure of a dance troupe's reputation.

Fish catchers and fish traders did not invest much in producer goods other than nets and canoes. It was ostentation, even hedonistically conspicuous consumption, that enabled one to cut a good figure at the carnival. Clothing was expensive, and carnival officers wore uniforms that Louis XIV might have admired. Dancers were decked in the finest wax prints (batiks) that money or influence could obtain, and alcohol was important in winning friends and supporters. Beer had to be hoarded well in advance for carnival, and sugar that would be surreptitiously distilled into cane rum had to be bought at bootleg prices in the townships. The old sixteenth-century Jaga custom of topping palm trees for palm wine was revived, much to the grief of farming communities that grew palm trees on the coastal plain. A skilled peasant knew how to tap a tree prudently to gain a modest but long-term supply of wine sap, but in the 1980s the palm groves of the Luanda plain were decimated by foraging speculators with a ready market for carnival palm wine but no thought for the morrow.

Despite its wealth, the prestigious Union of 54 did not win the 1987 carnival. The gods were displeased. The sea became rough. The canoes could not put out. The omens needed to be read again and the water gods had to be propitiated. The whale remained the fisherman's friend and was expected to bring messages, while the sirens so vividly described in 1620 remained a vibrant feature of life in the beach villages. If household gods and water deities could not remedy social and commercial failure, more drastic measures had to be taken. Forty miles down the coast the shrine of the chief priest of the sea god was in a baobab tree. It was there that the priest accepted offerings of expensive whiskey, port wine, and sweetmeats, all laid out on a fine tablecloth. When even the gods could not remedy a carnival failure, the law was taken into the hands of the hard men and gangs were sent out to gain revenge from opponents.

A more prosaic explanation of why the Union of 54 failed to win the competition was that its closest rival, the Union of N'Zumba, whose presence had traditionally spurred the Union of 54 on to greater prowess, did not participate, and a new rival, Island World, had gained in standing. Long based on the same beach as the Union of 54, the Union of N'Zumba had recruited its followers among the same elite families of the fishing aristocracy. It lost many supporters in the 1950s, however, when white immigrants took over the coast and drove black Africans to settle a few hundred yards inland in the Prenda quarter of the city. In the 1980s the group was still in financial crisis and, fearing a loss of status, withdrew from competitive dancing. The Union of N'Zumba attempted to recover its influence by sponsoring a football team, but even football was no match for a dance troupe. Island World's members belonged to the seamen's union. On trips abroad they could buy costumes that far outshone the drab government-issue textiles. By origin also a fisherman's union like the Union of 54,

Island World used the same varina style of dance. Of the six types of dance displayed at the carnival, the varina was the one that thrilled the shoreline crowds, and it was Island World that won the competition.

The economic influence of the fishing communities and the dominance of the varina dancers did not mean that other boroughs of the city were excluded from the carnival competition. Inland carnival groups had their own dance traditions and aspirations. *Kazukuta* was the dance style of the old proletarian quarter of the upper city. It flourished in the Bairo Operário, built early in the twentieth century as the residential zone for a declining black elite that had been driven out of the city center by white immigrants. The new suburb gained a twilight reputation for managing the informal sector of the city economy with unusual finesse. The borough was supposed to be a residential showpiece of colonial town planning, but the roads were never paved and the poets of Angola's protest literature decried the lack of electric light. Beyond the Bairo Operário lay Sambizanga, a poorer quarter for working-class black people. Here too the carnival dance tradition was kazukuta, but the passion for carnival was equaled, if not surpassed, by the passion for football. It was in the hungry slums of Sambizanga, under the cloak of a local football management committee, that the revolution of the dispossessed broke out in 1977. Since then security had been tight, and young soldiers were everywhere.

The attitude of the carnival to the soldiers was ambiguous. The conscripts were the children of the slums, and it was to the slums that they returned for safety when desertion seemed to be the only escape from eternal national service. The soldiers were also the champions of freedom, the people's militia, the protection against the vividly remembered foreign invasions from north and south that had so nearly captured the city on November 10, 1975. But the soldiers were also the arm of authority, and they brought fear to the slums. It was soldiers who crushed the popular uprising of 1977, who threatened the lucrative trade in bootleg spirits, who spied on black-market contraband, who had the guns to commit daylight robbery, and who sometimes held up law-abiding citizens on dark nights. Carnival in 1987 was still, as it was in colonial times, about exorcising the fear of authority.

The nominal heroes of the Angolan revolution and liberation were the peasants, but their participation in the carnival was meager. They sent only one group to the final competition to dance the *kabetula* dance of the farmers. To the big spenders of the fishing community, farming seemed a poor way of life. Even the great farms of the Bengo river, which sponsored *dizanda* dancers, sent only two competitive groups. Yet coastal farming was a growth sector of the Luanda economy. When government failed to maintain the living standards of the provinces and lost control of rural Angola to a rebellious peasant movement, the capital city underwent a crisis. The popular response was to bypass the bureaucratic structures of production and distribution and create a dynamic if informal free-market economy. New peri-urban farmers turned wasteland into cassava fields and tomato gardens. Parallel markets sprang up at which everything from champagne and television sets to canvas shoes and transistor batteries could be bought or sold or exchanged. Carnival groups, like everyone else in Luanda, learnt to juggle with state controls, seize market opportunities, and function with a two-tier exchange rate with unprecedented fiscal distortion.

Carnival is at heart a celebration. Politicians would have liked it to be a celebration of their strength and their popularity, but it was not. It was a celebration of ingenuity and survival: survival in a war without end, a war that began as a colonial war in 1961 and became a civil war in 1975. It was a celebration of the identity in which people rejoiced—not a national identity, not even a city identity, but an identity with neighbors and kinfolk in the closest, safest community that they could preserve. It was a celebration of wealth, of ostentatious display, of purchasing power, of conspicuous consumption. It was a celebration of freedom and a challenge to the awesome figures of authority that trespassed across the historic stage and had to be brought low by allegorical displays and carefully ritualized mockery. It was a celebration of youth in which grandmothers paraded the offspring of their daughters with pride and finery. It was a celebration of defiance before the perplexed bourgeoisie in a city bursting with class conflict. Above all, carnival was a celebration of historical tenacity and endurance. Five centuries of fishermen absorbed and tamed peoples, cultures, religions, and rituals from all over the world and made them a part of their very own Luanda carnival.

10

The Struggle for Power

In addition to a colonial war (1961–74) and an international war (1975–91), the history of Angola was darkened by two civil wars that pitted two surviving liberation movements against one another. The MPLA and UNITA fought each other mercilessly in both 1992–94 and 1998–2002. A History of Postcolonial Lusophone Africa *(2002), edited by Patrick Chabal, carried three chapters on Angola: one on the wars of the 1970s, one on the war of the 1980s, and a third on the wars of the 1990s. The third chapter is reprinted here by kind permission of the publishers, Christopher Hurst and Indiana University Press.*[1]

When Angola emerged from the cold war in 1991, it was a different country from the one that had emerged from the colonial war in 1974. In 1974 the major export had been coffee, efficiently carried by truck on asphalted highways built for strategic purposes. In 1991 one of the exports that exceeded coffee was scrap metal, quarried from the half a million tons of nonferrous junk attached to thousands of military and civilian vehicles that had been blown up during the years of bitter conflict and left along Angola's ruined roads. The graveyard of military vehicles was matched by the graveyard of human victims. Those who had died—of hunger, wounds, disease, or gunshots—were buried and uncounted, but those who survived—maimed, crippled, displaced, and unemployed—were all too visible and had to be counted by the agencies that supplied them with basic meals and artificial limbs. The war of destabilization, begun on the southern plain in the early 1980s, had spread through the highlands and lowlands until conflict reached Angola's northern frontier by the later 1980s. Only the larger urban enclaves of the highlands and the cities strung along the Atlantic shore were spared day-to-day fighting. Even these cities, however, felt the rigorous consequences of war when hundreds of thousands of war victims emerged from the countryside to seek refuge from the trauma that had engulfed all of village Angola.

It would be too simplistic to say that the reason a southern army had moved through the countryside destroying everything in its path was in order to terrify rural Angola's peasants into accepting the rule of Savimbi and UNITA and rejecting the rule of dos Santos and the MPLA. Much of the success of the southern army had been due to widespread rural disaffection with the MPLA government, and a civil war had therefore gone in tandem with the cold war, the war of destabilization. The difficult initial struggle of the MPLA to gain and hold the capital city had meant that rural Angola had been neglected. One of the causes of the great uprising of 1977 had been the suggestion that unemployed urban youths should be dispatched to the country as work brigades to pick the unharvested coffee crop. The youths were alarmed at the prospect. Their dignity depended on being sophisticated urbanites with, despite their minimal amount of schooling, a taste for sharp dressing. To be sent to a countryside full of yokels and wild animals, not to mention magicians and poisonous snakes, would have been a terrifying experience. Their disdain for the countryside was shared by salaried workers in the city, who contemptuously described the people of the countryside as the "Bantu," vernacular-speaking rustics quite unlike themselves with their smooth Portuguese manners. The antagonism between the town and the countryside had paved the way for the war of the

1980s to spread like a bush fire from neglected province to neglected province. Regional distrust remained a dreadful burden as the nation sought a sustainable peace for the 1990s.

Burdensome though the legacies of war may have been, the eighteen months from May 1991 to September 1992 were the most spectacular months of optimism and freedom that Angola had ever witnessed. Savimbi and his entourage of generals moved down from the highlands and set up their opulent residential quarters in the Miramar district of Luanda, overlooking the palm-fringed bay. Thousands of highland refugees in the coastal cities loaded their meager possessions on their heads and set off for the interior to rediscover their villages and seek out their surviving relatives. International observers poured into the country to marvel at the peace process, at the new economic opportunities, at the adoption by Africa of a democratic procedure to settle differences. The political parties hired public relations firms to run sophisticated election campaigns on television stations, and the political leaders drew large crowds of cheering supporters to their rallies in the country's town squares. The representative of the United Nations, Margaret Anstee, flew everywhere in decrepit aircraft parsimoniously funded by the United States and courageously flown by intrepid Russians. She endeavored to harmonize the two partisan armies that were to be partly demobilized and partly integrated into a single national force. The euphoria of peace made supervised demobilization virtually impossible, however. The government conscripts vanished into civilian society, while the opposition ones were hidden away in provincial redoubts in case "the leader" should require their services later. The most obsolete of UNITA weapons were handed over to teams of international inspectors, but sophisticated military equipment was cached away in arms dumps strategically chosen around the provinces by Savimbi himself. On the government side a new security force, dressed in a sinister black costume, was armed and trained for action against civilians should circumstances lead to urban guerrilla warfare after the election. While people danced in the streets and vowed that war should never return to their land, the pragmatic power brokers of both sides made contingency plans.

When, after a year of blissful peace, Angola finally went to the polls to elect a parliament and a new president, the voters divided cleanly and clearly between the town and the countryside. The towns had more or less survived the war of destabilization on the basis of imported food paid for with oil revenue and supplemented by philanthropy from organizations across the world. The countryside had done much less well, having suffered a sharp loss of earning capacity following the collapse of the colonial infrastructure and the total failure of the Soviet-style economy to create any rural network that could purchase produce from the farmers or distribute to them essential commodities such as soap, salt, and cooking oil. In September 1992 the countryside voted for the opposition—for Savimbi and for change—while the towns voted for the government—for preferential economic treatment and for armed protection from the hungry raiders out in the rural areas. Some modification of the voting pattern was effected by historic or ethnic loyalties, but the UNITA leaders were greatly dismayed to find that some urban Ovimbundu, in both highland towns and coastal cities, had failed to support them in their election bid and had adopted the national townsmen's strategy of voting for the MPLA. Even more dismaying to Savimbi was the betrayal of the United States, which, to all intents and purposes, had promised him that if he stopped the war and went to the polls he would undoubtedly win the election. When Savimbi failed to win, by a clear margin of two to one in the parliamentary election and by a decisive if not absolute majority vote for dos Santos in the presidential election, he immediately went back to war. Western-style democracy had no consolation prizes for coming second in its first-past-the-post, winner-takes-all system of voting.

The civil war that broke out in Angola in November 1992 was quite different from the colonial war of 1961 and from the interventionist war of 1975 and its destabilizing aftermath in the 1980s. Those wars had been fought in the countryside and had only indirectly affected the towns. The defeated opposition in

1992 could do its electoral sums quite as effectively as any UN observer and recognized that it was in the urban heartlands that it had lost its bid for power through the ballot box. UNITA therefore set out to destroy those urban heartlands and to destroy a government that had proven itself totally unwilling to make any concessions to its opponents by offering a significant postwar redistribution of the economic spoils of the extractive economy. The civil war of 1992 first broke out in Luanda itself, triggered by UNITA's intransigent rejection of the election result but initially launched and pursued with vigor by the government. Within days the city had been violently cleansed of politicians unwilling to abandon Savimbi's cause. Worse still, the urban militias were given the license to settle old scores by attacking townsmen who were thought to have voted for UNITA. Savimbi refused any compromise solutions, recognizing that the presidential system—so attractive to him when he thought he could win— gave all power to the president rather than to the prime minister, the cabinet, or the elected parliament. Savimbi calculated that his only hope of gaining the power that he had craved almost pathologically since his student days in Switzerland was to seize it through the barrel of a gun.

The war of 1992 brought even heavier weapons to Angola than those used in previous wars, and in the new conflict the big towns of the interior—Huambo, Kuito, Malange—were severely damaged while their populations were almost starved. Savimbi no longer had support from South Africa, but he did have access to relatively cheap secondhand weapons bought, ironically enough, from the countries of the former Soviet empire. He discovered in particular that the huge republic of Ukraine, with fifty million people struggling to make a living, was willing to sell redundant military equipment and had an air cargo fleet with the capacity to fly weapons, ammunition, and fuel oil to makeshift airstrips hidden in the orchard savanna of eastern Angola. Payment for the new UNITA arsenal came from the wild digging of diamonds extracted from rivers of the interior and flown out through cloak-and-dagger channels to Antwerp, the Belgian capital of the diamond-cutting world. In the expensive business of modern war, fought with technologically sophisticated weapons that required imported ammunition, UNITA recognized that its diamond wealth could not compete with the ten-times-greater oil wealth of the Angolan government. In 1993 UNITA attacked the onshore oil installations at the mouth of the Congo River, either to deprive the MPLA of revenue or to capture an oil supply of its own. The oil port of Soyo temporarily fell into opposition hands, but ruptured storage tanks only caused massive pollution while the oil platforms on the ocean horizon were never at risk from military activity. By 1994 Savimbi was forced to recognize that his early military successes had exhausted his resources and could bring no immediate political victory. For long-term survival he needed to seek a truce on the best terms he could extract.

Ending the war proved a particularly intractable diplomatic challenge. Margaret Anstee, having orchestrated the election with aplomb, negotiated valiantly to win the peace as well, but it was not until late in 1994 that a new UN peacemaker, Alioune Beye, eventually secured a cease-fire in Lusaka. The accord generated none of the euphoria that had accompanied the peace signed at Bicesse in 1991. Savimbi showed his contempt for the unpalatable necessity of suspending hostilities by staying away from the signing ceremony. He had no desire to come face to face with Eduardo dos Santos, who had now outwitted him both in a patently free and fair election and in prolonged siege warfare, which had given him control of highland cities that Savimbi deemed his birthright. Savimbi retired to the small highland town of Bailundu to plot future political or military developments. Dos Santos returned from Lusaka to Luanda to consolidate his personal power by both political and financial means. Savimbi evaded all forms of peace monitoring by the United Nations and refused to demobilize under the terms of the Lusaka Accord. Dos Santos basked in his international acclaim as a peacemaker who now enjoyed almost unlimited western support for his government. But war remained the agenda on the horizon, and each side tried to provoke the other into being the first to break the Lusaka cease-fire and incur the international opprobrium of being the guilty party that returned Angola to civil war. In the highlands the cold hostility, neither war nor peace, lasted for four years. Meanwhile civil society had been changing down on the coast.

The end of the cold war and the signing of the 1991 peace at Bicesse in Portugal had brought important changes to the status and role of the churches in Angola. For fifteen years after independence, the state and its nominally Marxist-Leninist government had ignored the churches. Members of the Luanda political elite who had remained affiliated to religious congregations had used great discretion, almost secrecy, when attending church services. Even the Methodist Church, in which several eminent leaders, including Agostinho Neto himself, had been nurtured, received only minimal official toleration. In the 1990s the government moved away from its initial hostility, and an attitude of toleration gradually gave way to an actual wooing of the churches by the presidency. Although 90 percent of Angolans now belonged to a church, the political influence of the congregations remained weak and the churches proved incapable of preventing further outbreaks of war. No church actively advocated war, but none was openly willing to condemn the concept of "peace through victory," and church members were trapped by a loss of liberty and human rights that scarred Angolan society throughout the 1990s.

The largest and most united church was the Catholic Church, which, although it had historically been split between foreign missionaries who stood up for black colonial subjects and Portuguese bishops who stood up for the white colonial state, was nevertheless firmly structured around a single authoritative voice legitimized by Rome. The Protestant churches, although riven by contrasts of ideology, pastoral tradition, and ethnicity, might have expected to benefit from a folk memory of Catholics as supporters of empire and Protestants as anti-imperialists who gave succor to the liberation movements. Any such legacy of sympathy between nationalists and Protestants was eroded after independence, however, by growing government conservatism. The Luanda elite, attempting to rebuild the country's traditions of power and subordination, approved of the Catholic Church's authoritarian hierarchy, and the old colonial tradition of treating the Catholic hierarchy as the natural ally of government was revived at the end of the cold war. Traditional Protestants and the old independent churches of the Kimbanguists and the Tokoists were left fragmented on the margins of society, and it was a new Pentecostal religious tradition that provided a spiritual home for the victims of war who crowded once more into the coastal cities after the abortive peace of 1991.

Once the pannational Catholic Church had overcome the stigma of its reactionary legacy from the colonial era, its influence began to grow and it became an attractive symbol of power for those who wanted to be associated with the elite. But Catholics also began to match Protestants in dispensing charity to the dispossessed and listening to the voice of the voiceless, thus usurping the role of the Methodists, who had lost their heroic status as defenders of the oppressed and were now perceived by some as the traditional partners of an uncaring MPLA government. Their standing was further diminished when the government presumed on Methodist loyalty and gave Methodists fewer state resources with which to alleviate poverty than it gave to the Catholic Church, whose endorsement it solicited in the game of power politics. As the government wooing of the churches progressed, Christians were openly welcomed into membership in the once-atheist ruling party and dos Santos appointed church leaders to his privy council. But coopting church leaders into the establishment weakened rather than strengthened the congregations. In Angola no "peace and justice" commission was set up, no "truth and reconciliation" were attempted, no rehabilitation of social relations between former enemies took place, and the state remained in full control of everyday life. Church members who wanted their lives to be independent of the politics of clientship found that they could not subsist without compromise. Non-smoking and teetotaling Protestants who had been morally outraged by the government issue of rations of tobacco and alcohol could not refuse to receive their allocation, since it was only by selling perquisites on the wild market for one hundred times their posted price that state sector employees could realize the value of their salary substitute and buy all the real necessities of life. The impotence of dependency reached down through the ranks of society and turned everyone into a vassal of the MPLA. While church members were becoming dependent on the party, the party began using the church as a symbol of its own power and prestige. Eduardo dos Santos, the Soviet-trained technocrat, chose to have his son baptized as a Catholic and invited the Pope himself to celebrate Mass for the millions in a Luanda football stadium. During the war-torn 1990s this cohabitation between church and state handicapped the efforts of the churches to find a means of satisfying the intense popular desire for peace. It was not until mid-2000 that the churches finally began to cooperate, regardless of the wrath of Dos Santos, and bring the people out into the streets of the capital to demonstrate for peace. An interchurch congress on the rights and wrongs of entering into dialogue with the enemy, rather than allowing the war to drag on, finally broke the silence of fear, and an open public debate about Angola's future was launched.

One political initiative designed to prevent a renewed outbreak of war had occurred in 1997. As part of the search for a policy that would defuse the anger of the opposition and minimize the danger of a return to war, the president created a "government of national unity." A limited number of junior posts were offered to members of the southern elite who were willing to leave the highlands and join the ruling circle in Luanda. Some seventy UNITA members who had been elected to parliament in September 1992 moved to the comforts of the city and took their seats in the legislative chamber; seven of their leaders became ministers and vice ministers in a cabinet whose padded payroll also included sixty MPLA members. This low-key concession to power sharing was silently undermined, however, by the continuing rise of presidential authority. One of the most potent effects of the failure of the UN election of 1992 and of the catastrophic war that followed was the decision by the president to concentrate more power in his own hands. From being a single-party state with a disaffected opposition thinly scattered in the provinces and abroad, Angola became a presidential state in which power emanated from the palace. Dos Santos, like Louis XIV, built his palace on the outskirts of the restless city, safely removed from the fickle mob, and it was there that political decisions began to bypass government ministries, party cells, and state bureaucracies. Angola was no longer a "people's republic," and the president's huge, well-fortified presidential complex, the Futungo, ostentatiously resembled the extravagant luxury of Mobutu in Congo-Zaire rather than the austere highland hideouts in which Savimbi dodged from night to night to avoid capture or assassination by his many personal foes and political enemies. But for all the gilding on his cage, dos Santos was almost as much a prisoner as Savimbi. After 1992 he virtually ceased to travel around the country, and even when he visited his own capital city he went with a heavily armed guard. The caged president orchestrated a personality cult, which led to an extravagant adulation that constantly emphasized his image as the man of peace, in shining contrast to Savimbi, who was always portrayed as the man of war. The presidential court even suggested that dos Santos, who had been at war with his own people for twenty years, be nominated for the Nobel Peace Prize.

In 1998 the presidential personality cult reached a climax during a week-long birthday party for dos Santos. He ceremonially visited the restoration work on the seventeenth-century chapel of Our Lady of Muxima, he launched a regatta and a parachuting competition, he awarded new costumes to paramount chiefs, he unveiled a commemorative postage stamp, and he opened an exhibition on "protecting the sea and its riches," thereby showing his ultramodern concern for ecology and the environment while many of his human subjects went on starving. The country's horrific medical plight gave the president an opportunity to visit favored hospitals bearing gifts and seeking loyalty, to visit a leper colony and a camp for displaced children, to express solidarity with those who campaigned against polio or sustained the victims of AIDS. An American-style fundraising dinner was devoted to the rehabilitation of the victims of land mines, which his government had probably done as much as Savimbi's opposition to scatter over the country. Amidst the hopeless despair that presaged an imminent return to war, the week ended with gymnastics, sporting competitions, the cutting of a birthday cake, and the awarding of a Brazilian honorary degree to the president. The bread-and-circus fantasies were an attempt to overcome rising popular disaffection and an increasing fear of police surveillance. As the president became all-powerful, even the Luanda elders of the MPLA found themselves marginalized, as was demonstrated when a prime minister from the prestigious Van Dunem Creole family was humiliatingly made to carry the blame for government unpopularity. But while the people on the street saw the junketing and partying as an extravagant display of scandal and corruption in high places, the establishment in the bureaucracies saw hero worship as the necessary gateway to power and status on the fringes of the court. As money poured into the presidency without let or hindrance, the politics of clientship became ever more pronounced, and success depended on largesse.

The development of the untamed market economy in Angola had serious consequences for the middle class. The purchasing power of state salaries dwindled with rampant inflation, and bureaucrats were driven, like the displaced poor of the shanties, to live by their wits. Economic insecurity led to corruption, violence, and crime, which touched the lives of all sectors of society. As in many other parts of Africa, public servants had no choice but to spend their time and energy working at second jobs in the private sector and retaining their formal jobs in the public sector to ensure for themselves structural positions and state privileges rather than monetary or material reward. As public services withered away, only those who offered bribe money, preferably in American dollars, could obtain the necessary medicines or documents to survive. Under these circumstances clientship became at least as necessary as it had been under the Soviet-style economic system, but the *nomenklatura*, the privileged elite, had to find new ways of obtaining patrons. This need for a patron was most acute in Luanda, where the bourgeois cost of living was comparable to that in Tokyo and yet salaries ranged from an utterly derisory 200 to a merely inadequate 2,000 dollars per month. Members of parliament, police officers, senior civil servants, and army commanders all came to depend on the president in person, who had pockets deep enough to award those whom he favored an annual Christmas bonus that was sometimes as high as 25,000 dollars, the equivalent of ten years' salary for a junior government employee. The sweetening of those on whom the regime depended was matched by the crushing of those who might dissent. During 1998, as the expectation of a new civil war rose to a certainty, the presidential office increased the range of organizations that became dependent on its bounty and were therefore trapped into silent complicity. Benefactions were used both to minimize grassroots protest from the hungry slums, which profoundly feared a return to war, and to manipulate the factions that kept the traditional cadres of the MPLA in disputatious disarray.

One of the small institutionalized steps on the road to totalitarian presidentialism in Angola had been the creation in 1996 of the Eduardo dos Santos Foundation. The foundation was designed to implement a widespread policy of privatizing the assets of the state in order that they could be used to consolidate the power of the president rather than meet any of the more objectively assessed political needs of the nation. The idea was far from new; a similar transfer of state resources from democratically accountable local and central government to quasi-non-governmental agencies run by political favorites had already been undertaken on a large scale in Thatcher's Britain—"selling the family silver," as Harold Macmillan pithily called it. In Angola, however, the process was masked by rather more opaque layers of secrecy and cloaked in even more dubious forms of legality than any adopted in other countries. Privatization policies were politically motivated, designed to prevent the overthrow of the government either by democratic vote in the world's north or by mob restlessness in the countries of the less affluent south. In Angola the president's patrimonial foundation refined the politics of patronage by a further concentration of power in the Futungo palace. The funds of the foundation derived from a presidential "tax" that mirrored the state taxes levied on international trading firms, petroleum prospectors, construction companies, banking corporations, and small domestic businesses. Having creamed off a top slice of the nation's assets, the presidential foundation went into competition with the state to provide services that had ceased to be available through official channels but that now became privately accessible to the president's clients. A private presidential university was set up to compete with the underfunded downtown Agostinho Neto University, which subsequently saw both foreign finance and foreign personnel eroded. Even greater finesse was shown in the case of a home for abandoned children in the suburb of Cacuaco, for which the foundation gained public credit with a small subsidy while the core funding was siphoned out of the city of Luanda's own budget. Some of the largesse reached the provinces, but the presidential bounty was predominantly spent in the city, the political base with the greatest capacity to make or unmake presidents in the event of revolution.[2]

Manipulating power by offering carrots and showing sticks to the elite was rather easier than winning support among the urban masses, who saw poverty as the consequence of widespread corruption at the highest levels. It became necessary to generate "spontaneous" outbursts of popular enthusiasm for the president, but only authorized spontaneity could be tolerated. The restless workers of Sambizanga—the black parish in which the president had been born, but also the parish in which Nito Alves had mounted his 1977 challenge to the government of Agostinho Neto—were persuaded to come down into the asphalt town and demonstrate their loyalty to the president. The spontaneity had been so well prepared that the chanting crowds wore specially prepared T-shirts bearing pictures of "their" president. The mobilization of the dispossessed rapidly soured, however, when the crowds were permitted to search out approved public enemies against whom to vent their rage over their shabby poverty. The first permitted target was an ethnic one—the demonstrators chanted anti-Ovimbundu slogans as they intimidated anyone who had come down from the highland and might have UNITA sympathies. In order to separate out the faithful from the faithless, it was suggested in parliament that identity cards should be issued naming the "tribe" of each bearer, but this calamitous recipe for urban warfare was not carried out. By 1996 the orchestrated politics of violence were extended to include xenophobia, and crowds were permitted to attack anyone who might be branded as foreign. A government campaign against aliens was given the chilling code name "Cancer Two," and the search for enemies was directed not only at Africans, particularly "Zaireans" from Congo, but also at the communities of Lebanese and other Asian businessmen, whom the population saw as exploiters but whom the president's men now wished to supplant in the lucrative import-export sector of wholesale trade.

While corruption was being orchestrated by politicians down in the city, the highlands were getting ready for war. By the end of 1996 it was estimated that Savimbi's war chest had grown to two billion U.S. dollars and that he had recently been able to buy another 450 tons of weapons flown in from Bulgaria to the airstrip that UNITA conscripts had built near Bailundu. At this time no less than 20,000 of Angola's government troops were being tied down in Cabinda, where three armed secessionist movements were threatening the security of the oil wells. Each movement had the potential to secure active support from Angola's northern neighbors, Congo-Brazzaville and Congo-Zaire, either of which would gladly have conquered Cabinda. In May 1997 this foreign situation suddenly altered when the thirty-year-old dictatorship of Mobutu collapsed in Congo-Zaire and a new military dictator, Laurent Kabila, who had a shadowy past in the Lumumba era, took control of Kinshasa and entered into an alliance with the dos Santos government in Luanda. As a result of the change, some 10,000 of Savimbi's troops who had been sheltered by Mobutu in preparation for the next Angolan civil war found themselves temporarily stranded, and some tried to seek refuge in Congo-Brazzaville. Within a month of the Kinshasa revolution a similar revolution broke out in Brazzaville, followed by four months of a peculiarly savage civil war in which 10,000 townsmen were killed. To ensure that the outcome did not threaten its own security, Angola sent an army into Congo-Brazzaville and occupied the oil port of Pointe Noire. The troops also enabled General Sasso—with the tacit connivance of oil interests in both France and the United States—to overthrow the elected Brazzaville government despite mercenary interventions from new international players such as Uzbekistan and Croatia. The turbulence in Kinshasa and Brazzaville disrupted UNITA's war preparation, but during 1998 Savimbi retrieved his scattered units and some highly trained members of Mobutu's fleeing presidential guard and mobilized a force of 15,000 trained men and 10,000 auxiliary conscripts. He also recruited some of the genocidal Rwanda militants who were hiding in Congo-Kinshasa, some orphaned military companies that had lost out in the civil war in Brazzaville, and some Serbian mercenaries; and he commissioned Morocco to train a new officer corps for UNITA to replace those generals who had been handsomely seduced into moving to Luanda to set up a renegade UNITA faction in the city.

The dos Santos government prepared for war as actively as did UNITA in the months that followed the apparently accidental death of the UN peacekeeper Alioune Beye in June 1998. Thirty battalions were deployed around the country, and an air force equipped with Brazilian jets was put on standby near Benguela, ready to strafe the highlands. Spanish counterinsurgency specialists retrained 25,000 commandos in special police units prepared to repress any civilian unrest caused by war. The city politicians hoped quickly and definitively to drive UNITA's forces out of the country and into Zambia. The city generals aspired to capture the Kwango valley, where the most plentiful alluvial diamonds were to be found. In the last weeks of 1998 a section of dos Santos's army persuaded the president that any further delay in dealing a death blow to Savimbi's forces would be strategically foolish.

Savimbi had been arming so heavily, however, that it was already too late to strike a surprise winning blow. The government forces, inappropriately armed and inadequately trained, were fiercely repulsed when they tried to take the highlands. During the first half of 1999 UNITA held the military advantage, and even its reluctant recruits, kidnapped from nominally friendly Ovimbundu territory, fought for their lives, terrified that if they lost the war to the *mestiços* of the city they would be packed off to the lowlands as despised farm labor. The civil war of 1998 became the cruellest yet seen in Angola. UNITA starved the cities, notably Malange and Kwito, by refusing to allow humanitarian food supplies to be flown in by the international agencies. It hoped that the Angolan government would be forced by world opinion to stop a war that was killing thousands of civilians. Savimbi may also have hoped that the coast would rise up in revolt as new waves of displaced persons descended from the shattered highland towns. But the world, fascinated by the wealth of Angola's oil wells, did not press the government to negotiate a peace, and the civilians did not risk mounting any public protest when their streets were patrolled by black-clad security police.

The depraved war between a government mesmerized by wealth and an opposition obsessed by power carried on throughout 1999 and into 2000. In some successful engagements UNITA captured government weapons, but a shortage of fuel caused it serious logistical difficulties. One solution was to buy diesel covertly from dealers in the enemy camp. Personal relations across the divide between the two warring elites were much closer than ethnic or ideological enmity would have led one to suppose; successive peace negotiations had accustomed rival delegations to do business with one another while drinking together in expensive nightclubs staffed by the seductive hostesses of Abidjan or Lusaka. For UNITA to buy fuel on a black market run by enemy officers required a large supply of fresh diamonds, and in the late 1990s it was estimated that 100,000 men and women were being forced to dig the cold alluvial mud of the Kwango River for some of the world's most sought-after gem diamonds. Although Angola's di-

amonds earned only about one-tenth of the seven billion dollars
a year derived from oil, a significant proportion of them were mar-
keted by UNITA, bypassing official cartel channels licensed by
De Beers and enabling Savimbi to continue military operations
after cold war funding had ceased. With diamond money UNITA
leaders were able to win support from French client regimes in
Burkina Fasso, Togo, and Ivory Coast, all of which provided them
with travel documents. So much blood money became involved in
the sale of Angola's diamonds, as in the sale of those from Sierra
Leone, that the United Nations imposed penalties on nations that
facilitated the diamonds-for-weapons trade. At the same time De
Beers feared that if it did not stop the diamond cutters and pol-
ishers from buying bargain-price diamonds from war zones, the
world might mount a humanitarian campaign against the wearing of diamonds similar to the one that animal rights activists
had used to make the wearing of furs socially unacceptable in western society. Despite all the protests, guns were still flown into
highland Angola under cover of darkness, carried by mercenary
planes using unsupervised airstrips in countries that were re-
warded for closing their eyes. The crisis in diamond sales from
Angola became acute only when it was realized that the government supply of legitimate diamonds, dug from a deep-level kim-
berlite mine, was being enhanced by conflict diamonds that free-
wheeling generals were buying from their cash-strapped opponents
and legitimizing with forged certificates of provenance. President dos Santos, whose daughter held a diamond-dealing license,
had to act to make sure that Angolan diamond licenses were
above any suspicion of forgery, which might have closed down
the industry on both sides of the war zone. As oil prices fell temporarily to ten dollars a barrel, the government was almost as
anxious as UNITA to protect diamond export revenues. Although the MPLA had written off four billion of its eleven billion
dollars of old war debts, it had been forced, at a time when oil
prices were dropping, to buy hugely expensive new weapons with
which to conduct the war of 1998. When oil prices recovered, the
military tide turned, UNITA lost its highland headquarters in

Bailundu, and the fighting was once more concentrated in the dry, empty plains on the borders of Zambia, through which Savimbi moved in his mobile command caravan visiting his shifting guerrilla camps.

The international scramble to obtain a stake in the Angolan oil industry reached gold-rush proportions. The giant exploration companies, those of Britain and France to the fore, calculated that the North Sea and Alaskan fields would run out of viable new reserves in the new century and that it was in the ultradeep concessions off Angola's Atlantic coast that the best prospects were to be expected. Although drilling oil from a seabed two miles deep called for a technology that had not yet been perfected, with underwater stations serviced by automated submarines and flexible extraction pipes attached to surface platforms out in the ocean, the companies were willing to make down payments of 300 million dollars for the right to explore each concession block in Angola's deep waters. In the early months of the new millennium, Luanda's "jungle capitalism," to use Tony Hodges's felicitous phrase, was once more awash with money.[3] The benefits, however, did not trickle down to the people. Schoolteachers continued to be outnumbered two-and-a-half to one by soldiers, while the elite spent a generous share of the national education budget on sending its children abroad to obtain a sound education. Voices of complaint, including that of the editor of the one significant independent news sheet in Luanda, were silenced, apparently by MPLA death squads, much as newspapermen had previously been murdered in Huambo by UNITA death squads. In the countryside the totalitarian savagery of UNITA continued unabated with the kidnapping of all available children for military duty and the burning of dissidents after accusations of witchcraft. While the slaughter went on in the highlands, members of Savimbi's own family sheltered in a haven of exile controversially afforded to them by the West African president of the Republic of Togo. In the city oil continued to be the fuel that inflamed civil war, as it had been since the dawn of independence on November 11, 1975.

By the year 2000 Angola had come full circle in the thirty years since the death of Salazar, Portugal's old dictator. The civil wars of the 1990s, like the colonial wars of the 1960s, had reached a stalemate. The lives of many people were disrupted, but no solution to the military confrontation between the central system of government and the guerrillas on the periphery seemed in sight. The economy had changed from a dependence on the fluctuating price of coffee to a dependence on the equally unpredictable price of petroleum. In neither case was the industrial sector of production able to cushion the country significantly against the uncertainties of the world market for raw commodities. Politics in 2000 was as unresponsive to public opinion as it had been in 1969, though the dictator who balanced the powers of the several factions of the property-owning class was now a member of the homegrown Luso-African elite of Luanda rather than the imperially oriented haute bourgeoisie of fascist Portugal. In each case the army kept an eye on political decision making and a finger in the economic pie. Senior officers in the colonial army of the 1960s built their wealth on a black market underpinned by coffee exports and currency speculation and invested it in real estate in Lisbon. In the national army of the 1990s officers dominated the now-privatized trade in diamonds and invested their wealth in the Luanda housing market, earning large fortunes as landlords to the foreign employees of oil companies, diplomatic missions, and philanthropic aid agencies. Wealth was as sharply polarized in 2000 as it had been in late colonial times, but the city slums had grown from half a million established members of the *musseque* families to four million displaced transients camped on the Luanda coastal plain. The colonial class of three hundred thousand privileged and semiprivileged expatriates had been replaced by a similar number of black Portuguese-speaking Angolans who retained many of the old colonial attitudes of social and moral superiority and worshipped in the same Catholic churches that had sustained Salazar's brand of authoritarianism. On the streets the Angolan press of the 1990s was as circumscribed in its news and opinions as ever the censored press of the 1960s had been, and Angolan citizens who held political views were as wary of the political police as colonial subjects had been when trying to evade Salazar's secret agents. Freedom of opinion and of opportunity, which had been stifled in the days of empire, proved virtually incapable of resuscitation in the era of liberation.

11

A Journey through Angola

In May 2003 I was invited to accompany four members of a British parliamentary delegation to Angola. This personal account of some of the things we saw and heard represents a background to the official all-party report.[1] It also draws on the short piece published in the house journal of the Royal Institute of International Affairs, whose staff, attached to the British Angola Forum, organized the visit. Our purpose was to witness the reconstruction and resettlement being attempted in both urban and rural Angola one year after the end of the series of wars chronicled in this book. I am very grateful to Hilton Dawson, Andrew Robathan, Tony Colman, and Francis Listowel for their companionship; their indefatigable professionalism quite restored my faith in politicians.

The most unexpected aspect of postwar Angola in May 2003 is the vibrancy of the free press. Every Saturday the streets of the *cidade asfaltada* (asphalt city) are alive with runners selling no less than five titles. The competition is fierce as editors struggle to devise ever more eye-catching stories of financial malfeasance and political infighting. The most noted, and most persecuted, of the weeklies so suffered from the strain that some of its editorial board members left and two rival papers are now on the street: the *Angolense,* number 226, boasting its sixth year of survival, and the *Semanário Angolense,* number 11, in its first year of publication.

Government attempts at curbing the explosion of pent-up frustrations that seethe among the cultured Angolan middle classes have been a mixture of the crude and the subtle. The attempt at direct prepublication censorship seems to have backfired. When political newspapers appeared with blank spaces, reader curiosity knew no bounds and samizdat photocopies of offending articles, which had often previously appeared in the Portuguese press, were passed from hand to hand through business and government offices. Editors seem not to have adopted the ingenious scam of the old *Central African Examiner,* which, in the first days of Ian Smith's Rhodesian rebellion, offered prizes to readers who correctly filled in the censor's blank spaces. The government in Luanda backtracked on censorship, not having the skills of the old Salazar dictatorship, which filled blank spaces with government copy tailored to fit the gaps. More covert forms of pressure are therefore applied by latter-day minders of the public consciousness.

The big story, which has run and run, is "Who are the richest men in Angola?" The names and photographs of the fifty-nine top candidates are now very much in the public domain. Each is allegedly worth more than fifty million United States dollars, some of them more than one hundred million. The list may not be very accurate either in names or in magnitudes, but its publication has had very interesting consequences. One Angolan entrepreneur took the offending newspaper to court and charged it with destroying his credit rating on the international financial markets. He was, he protested, worth very much more than the alleged one hundred million dollars he was accused of siphoning off the common weal. The paper's editor also went to court and accused the government of libel. The official press, he said, had so intemperately denounced the millionaire story as a slur on the integrity of members of the ruling elite that it had undermined his reputation for journalistic probity. The government, whose supporters featured prominently on the list, referred the story to the attorney general, but he very publicly washed his hands of the matter and passed the case to the criminal police. The destination of Angola's three billion dollars' worth of missing oil earnings is one of the fascinating facets of a new stirring of public awareness.

The defining moment of Angola's loss of innocence came a generation ago, on May 27, 1977. When the younger folk in Luanda feel reasonably safe from the prying ears of the security services, they ask ever more insistently, "Daddy, where were you on May 27?" In a country where most women are politically marginalized, they might even ask mother where she was hiding while the blood flowed in the prisons. The pervasive fear of "preventive detention," which normally reduces freedom of speech to mere freedom of conversation, is based on folk memory of the extensive witch hunts that followed the 1977 attempt by young idealists, including some radical young women, to overthrow pragmatic male graybeards. That was the day when the Angolan dream began to unravel. That was when the old president's cancer began to take a terminal hold. That was when old scores between guerrilla factions were resolved. That was when freedom died. It is therefore astonishing to find the free press in Luanda carrying an old speech by Nito Alves, the martyred hero of the impetuous young who had planned the rebellion of 1977 under the cloak of managing the Sambizanga football club—doubly astonishing since the working-class suburb of Sambizanga, focus of subversion in the popular mind, has once again been without water for five days in May 2003 and people are thirsty, dirty, and cross.

The memory of 1977 remains vivid, tragically refreshed in the autumn of 1992, when Luanda witnessed another bloodbath. In that year the old cold war veteran Jonas Savimbi, the man of violent passions, of towering arrogance, of fiery oratory, had been assured by the United States that if only he would submit himself to a democratic election he would surely gain the power that had eluded him for twenty-six long years. But he and his American sponsors did not win. He was worsted at the polls by the gray José Eduardo dos Santos, whom the voters deemed the less fearsome of the presidential candidates. Savimbi cried foul, but even the most brilliant of psephologists could never have devised a rigged result as complex, surprising, sophisticated, and varied as the verdict given by the people of Angola when they turned out in their full millions to take part in the country's one and only general election. It was back to the gun for Savimbi, but before he could strike the government launched a virulent preemptive blow. Those too young to remember the killings of 1977 vividly remember the killings of 1992, and when conversation in public places turns to politics local people fall eerily silent. As the embassy's armored car, with its Gurkha backup, drives me through the night city to the airport, key points of that urban war are pointed out. At notorious intersections cars thought to contain opposition sympathizers had been stopped, the occupants shot, and the vehicles set ablaze. Ten years later, when peace was finally signed over Savimbi's remote grave at the end of the earth, the remnants of his UNITA movement donned three-piece suits and moved into the city. The leaders began to seek a coherent political purpose and to use the new columns of the independent weekly press.

Freedom of the press may irritate the Angolan government, but it does not really threaten it. The newspapers are far too expensive for most ordinary salaried workers, and the expatriate business and diplomatic corps is not sophisticated enough to read between the editorial lines. The real requirement for the building of an open society, a civil society, a democratic society, an informed society is the radio. It was radio that got the nationalist movements up and running in Angola in the 1960s; it was a broadcasting station that was the focus of confrontation between the coup leaders of 1977 and the Cuban expeditionary force, which silenced their microphones; it was UNITA's Voice of the Black Cockerel that kept Savimbi's name alive during the civil wars. In 2003 the capacity and willingness of the Catholic Church to finance and shelter a radio station that asked impertinent questions causes the government qualms, and occasionally bishops have to go to the Bunker to apologize to the president's men. In this power game embassies play an interesting role. At one level an embassy is there to ensure that business contracts fall to its home country's citizens, though in truth only Portugal and Brazil have the cultural and linguistic fluency to score well at this game. The other role of an embassy is a mildly subversive one as diplomats daily test the democratic temperature. In this game the powerless patronize the diplomatic cocktail circuit to discuss political openness and fiscal transparency with hosts who are excluded from the closed magic circle of Luanda's power brokers. The newfound voices of "civil society" provide a glimmer of hope that politics may change; if these voices could gain access to broadcasting, debate might really become a part of the political scene. But when the 2003 parliamentary delegation from Britain visited a church radio station, its members found a palace general waiting for them in the editor's office.

The parliamentary visitors of 2003 are met at midnight by a formally attired ambassador who begins their briefing in the VIP lounge at Luanda airport while efficient airport minions expedite luggage and paperwork. And so through lit but potholed streets to the Tropico Hotel, lavishly rebuilt home of visiting oil executives, diamond smugglers, Bretton Woods bankers, and opposition turncoats and the drinking hole for all the semiwealthy flotsam of the asphalt lower city who wish to keep their ears tuned to the groundswell of political and financial gossip. Next morning the pink dawn rises as the uniformed flunkeys change the guard at the portico and the street urchins urgently skip up and down the dual carriageway selling newspapers through car windows to commuters. Government policy seems to be a question of how to enlarge the begging bowl and get people around the table for a so-called donor's conference. This agenda is apparently in direct contradiction to the policies of the several hundred nongovernmental agencies that help keep Angola's nose above water level, and whose desire is to devise exit strategies that will leave government to staff and fund the social rehabilitation program that the world's voluntary sector has initiated. Aid fatigue is seen to be imminent. Advisers to government recognize that if fiscal transparency is not improved and the $740 million-a-year leakage of oil revenues to private offshore investments is not stemmed, the world will wash its hands of Angola, starvation or no starvation. The organization Transparency International ranks Angola number 124 in its Corruption Perceptions Index.[2] The country may be rich, but the people are very poor.

Along the once-colonial streets of Luanda's lower town the divide between the haves and the have-nots is conspicuous as one passes the bored excombatants standing as armed guards by the iron grills of parlors where the beautiful ones are having their bouffant hairstyles refreshed. But lift your eyes up to the new De Beers skyscraper and you are liable to fall through a sewage manhole with a broken cover or be crowded by a chauffeur-driven six-cylinder saloon skirting months of accumulated street rubbish. The policeman pirouetting on his upturned tub still directs traffic with a deft flick of the wrist in front of the city hall, while elsewhere intermittent electric traffic lights control chaotic drivers and pedestrians at crowded intersections. The once-ubiquitous taxis with green fenders, symbols of lower-middle-class well-being, have vanished, and those who do not have cars line up for rusting privatized buses. Beyond the city the roads to and from the provinces are overburdened with worn-out trucks straining to carry oversized cargoes across makeshift bridges.

In between the tinted Mercedes owner and the matriarchal onion hawker it is difficult to find the voice of middle-class Angola. Especially if you are a mere Briton. One hundred years ago the British ruled Luanda, or at least the service sector and the import-export business. Now Victoria's Portuguese stepchildren have taken over, and self-respecting Angolans do business only with the best—the Portuguese, the former grandmasters, the imperialists whom the nationalists have tamed, the devils whom everyone knows and trusts. Any foreigner who is not Portuguese is mildly despised in Angola's profoundly neocolonial political culture. When an ambassador throws a dinner party, he cannot predict who will turn up: a hungry excombatant, a marginalized politician in a tight-fitting suit, a local functionary hoping to find a bursary. A few articulate agency voices call themselves the "civil society," but their unifying agenda was the call for peace, and now that the guns in all but the ultrarich oil enclave of Cabinda have ceased thundering, the civil society has lost some of its cohesion of purpose. The clearest vision of a new future may come from women, but in Angola the macho pecking order remains very Latinized. The bronze figure of the seventeenth-century Queen Nzinga may stand on the pedestal where Agostinho Neto once commanded the entrance to the Avenue of the Old Veterans, but this symbolism is not reflected in twenty-first-century gender politics.

The enclave of downtown Luanda, with its political intrigue, its sexual gossip, its irrelevant cocktail parties, its billion-dollar loan sharks, is not Angola. To visit the real Angola, removed from the suffocating obsession with power and wealth, you need to travel five or ten miles from the center, beyond the end of the old colonial tarmac. Suddenly you are immersed in a vibrant world of free-market dynamism that is probably as energetic and inventive as any economic system in the world. It has had to be if people and politicians alike were to survive the bizarre distortions that a soi-disant Marxist system of command economics imposed on the country in the 1980s. The survival strategies that women merchants and male artisans developed in those years now serve the country exceedingly well. The hundred-acre open-air work-shops are hives of industry where there is virtually nothing that cannot be made or bartered by Angolans of incredible ingenuity. When local supplies of recycled scrap fail, raw materials come in on the oil budget, plywood from the plundered forests of Indonesia, calico from the cotton mills of Congo, roofing nails from the iron furnaces of Europe. A Heath Robinson (what Americans might call a Rube Goldberg) diesel generator has been hauled in by a shrewd speculator who sells power through a web of tangled cables to hundreds of open-air carpenters making every conceivable item of furniture or style of roofing timber, not to mention fleets of wooden wheelbarrows. The metals section of the market is filled with blacksmiths who can turn wrecked cars into workshop tools or domestic utensils. Portly businesswomen sit under huge colored umbrellas selling everything from small brass screws to heavy headloads of cotton prints displayed at a dollar a yard. Up on the cliff, beyond the great workshops, the thousand-acre market known as Tira Bikini will have the bikini off your back and resell it before you can bat an eyelid. There the market women reach far beyond the neighboring countries of Central Africa and wholesalers have tentacles that stretch from Brazil to Dubai. There is nothing that cannot be bartered, be it a window motor for your air-conditioned Mercedes or half a gross of plastic sandals to be hawked through the township alleyways.

There are difficulties to be overcome in this wild world of free enterprise. Death from disease stalks stallholders and customers alike when they work all day in beating sun with neither a water supply nor a latrine for miles around. The big social insurance associations are the ones concerned with funeral expenses, which might at any moment suddenly impose great financial burdens on any small family firm. But savings systems for community tragedies are not the only form of inventiveness that Angolans have had to develop. The currency system also requires skill and experience. At the height of the "Marxist" experiment prices were calculated in six-packs of lager and wealth was stored in commodities rather than currencies. Now the home for a market woman's cash is the American dollar. Money changers take their cut, but when inflation runs at about 100 percent, stallholders prefer to change their money back and forth, if necessary every week, to preserve value while at the same time having the liquidity for daily transactions in local bundles of banknotes. The system works—Angolans are shrewd and competent businesspersons—but of late the government has been trying to put its oar in and an intrusive agency, the "fiscal police," is making urban survival more difficult, more dangerous, more needful of ingenuity.

There are some surprises in this world of unbridled capitalism. In a country where more than 40 percent of the black population speaks Portuguese as its preferred language and where many people barely think of themselves as Africans at all, it turns out that adult education in the market suburb is being conducted in French. When a stranger visits a technical college classroom his words of greeting are translated not into the local Kimbundu but into the Lingala lingua franca of western Congo. Enterprise in Greater Luanda often remains in the hands of networks of people who gained their commercial experience either as emigrants during the colonial heyday or as refugees during the colonial and postcolonial wars. The children of returnees from Kinshasa, the Congo metropolis where French is the language of government and Lingala the language of the marketplace, have not yet been reabsorbed into the Lusophone culture of their ancestral homeland.

The four million provincial migrants who have settled around Greater Luanda during the four successive wars that tore the country apart with ever-increasing virulence are not all engaged in business and bustle. Some of them live in tented cities of unspeakable poverty and deprivation, and even the majority who are sheltered by cement-block walls and corrugated roofs have no access to standpipes for their water and no system of sanitation more sophisticated than squatting behind a bush—as the actor Joseph Fiennes discovered when making a publicity film for Christian Aid. This is where the white Land Rover brigade comes into its own. Building public latrines that market stallholders and their customers can use for a penny a visit really is a service that can immediately reduce levels of disease and infection and ought to open the way for a system of local government that actually provides services. One organization goes even further and has devised a prototype system of municipal refuse collection, using old oil drums on swivel sticks that can easily be emptied into a cart drawn by an agency tractor. In Kilamba Kiaxi, where the baobab stands under which the founding hero of the nation allegedly wrote up his plan for a liberation war, municipal seminars are held at which people publicly speak out on the subject of latrines and refuse collection. The memory of Agostinho Neto makes the place where this first forum was held into hallowed ground to which politicians, and even the old hero's widow herself, come to drink at the fonthead of political wisdom. The idea of holding local debates might—or might not—catch on in less privileged places and become the beginning of participatory democracy in a city accustomed to the old Portuguese practice of rule by fascist decree. Sooner or later elections will be held, and meeting the newly expressed demand for public service could be good for electoral advantage.

Water is the big political issue in Luanda. Historically the city sent canoes up the coast to the nearest river to bring down more or less drinkable water. Nowadays water is privately distributed by tanker truck to all except the privileged few who receive it, effectively cost free though sometimes only intermittently, by municipal pipe. The cost of water is normally about a penny a liter, but in one camp, to which beggars and their dependents had been banished to prettify the downtown area, the price jumped several-fold when a storm washed a bridge away and the tankers had to make a detour along unreliable mud paths. Even at the best of times water from the entrepreneur who owns the truck may cost a family half of its combined weekly income. Thus it is that another very welcome foreign initiative is the laying of suburban pipelines to the shanty towns, sometime with small decoy pipes laid above the main ones so that when water robbers, who belong to an industry that earns $35 million a year, try to tap into the supply to fill their trucks they will only siphon water from the minor pipe and not destroy the pressure in the heavy-duty mains.

Nightmares are not confined to that half of the population living in cities of displaced persons strung along the coast. The wheeling and dealing of black marketeers may have enabled the swollen coastal slums to survive, but no such options were available in the provinces. Both the third war (1992–94) and the fourth war (1998–2002) were designed to starve and destroy whole populations. The victims of the third war still live in the shells of cities that had been blasted by UNITA for failing to vote for Savimbi in the electoral beauty contest of 1992. Huambo, the highland city built between the 1920s and 1960s as the Benguela railway workshop and the hub of a planter economy, remains shattered, although a road up from the coast is now navigated by intrepid truckers and a road down from the interior has been cleared by the Halo Trust, an international mine-disposal agency. A year after the peace was signed, survivors still huddled in encampments over which the ruling party hoisted its partisan flag of victory rather than a national flag of reconciliation. Opposition regiments are being demobilized, though not with quite the care that had been promised in the form of resettlement kits, tools, seeds, and blankets, let alone any training for civilian jobs. Even the limited support given to former combatants was reserved for men, and little recognition was afforded to the women who had been enrolled into the armies to provide every variety of domestic, portering, and sexual service to the boys in the bush. As for children in army service, the government refused to recognize their existence or to grant them demobilization papers. Adolescents remain at risk, after being informally demobilized, of being formally mobilized all over again when they reach conscription age. They fear the city generals sent up from the coast to rule the wilderness.

Only four million of Angola's people live in Luanda. The other ten million do not, and they have not had a good war. In the colonial war (1961–74) many of their fathers and mothers were conscripted as ultracheap labor to work for a pittance on settler farms and in the mines. When city politicians, both in government and in opposition, dream about a golden past flowing with milk and honey and rich in coffee and diamonds, rural people become apprehensive. In the cold war (1975–91) matters got worse and conscripted peasants had to serve whichever army caught them first, to do the bidding of Moscow and Havana or of Washington and Pretoria. The first civil war (1992–94) was more murderous again, though this time it was towns that were destroyed, particularly the highland cities that had "betrayed" Savimbi by voting to join ranks with the wealthy urban elites on the coast. By the time of the second civil war (1998–2002) survival strategies were wearing thin and the eternal optimism for which Africa is noted was becoming threadbare. It was this last war that caused the greatest distress to farmers on the wide eastern plains. Along the upper Zambezi peasants had been compelled to feed UNITA irregulars, and so the Luanda government bluntly decided to starve half a million people across the whole region to make sure that there was no food that the "bandits" could steal. Such brutal policies caused some farming families to flee to Zambia in search of vacant common land on which to subsist. The lucky ones found employment on Zambian farms or were sheltered in refugee camps sustained with flour, beans, cooking oil, and salt by the World Food Program. The less fortunate offended their hosts by accepting menial ill-paid jobs that undercut the wage-bargaining power of local Zambian laborers.

Now that the war is over, people from the Zambian camps are moving back to the small towns inside the Angolan border and activity is beginning to hum in the villages. Two hundred children in a country-town orphanage, half of them resident in double bunks with mosquito nets and half coming in from local families where they have been socially placed, start the day by raucously singing a Portuguese adaptation of the old song "If you're happy and you know it clap your hands, if you're happy and you know it nod your head, if you're happy and you know it—and you *really* want to show it—stamp your feet. . . ." Each verse has vigorous gestures, and when it is led by a British earl and a Labour parliamentarian the shining faces of the children are marvelous to behold. If infant mortality in Angola is to be reduced, many more mosquito nets will be needed and government will have to change some of its spending priorities to supply the chemicals to treat them. If the half of Angola's children who get no schooling at all are to be enrolled in classes such as the orphanage provides, education budgets will have to be introduced into all eighteen provinces.

Although peace finally arrived in 2002, the peace dividend appears to be spent in town rather than spread across the provinces. Since half of all Angola's people are children, the biggest peacetime demand is for education. Those within reach of a school find conditions Spartan: blackboard and chalk, one teacher for each hundred new entrants, very few textbooks, no exercise books. One such school, with an enthusiastic enrolment of pint-sized tots, was reached by Britain's parliamentary visitors after they had crossed the swollen Zambezi in a very small dugout canoe. The school, together with a small leper colony, is being supported by an evangelical aid agency. Elsewhere Unicef is making up for forty lost years in a country where parents had sometimes gained a little colonial schooling but the children of the war are illiterate. In the two heartland provinces of Malange and Huambo, 250,000 children need schools and several thousand teachers need training. Now that the war is over, however, every adult who did not manage to get to the coastal cities as a refugee hopes to get there as a job seeker. No Angolan, whether a teacher or any other ambitious citizen, wants a posting to the countryside. Urban drift is universal, not simply a feature of war.

If education is one responsibility that government cannot indefinitely delegate to philanthropic agencies, health is another. As exiles test the viability of a return to their ancestral villages, the question of health provision will be much on their minds before they bring parents and children home to Angola. The task of providing even minimal care in communities of returnees will be made difficult by bureaucratic obstructionism. The qualifications gained by Angolans in Congo or in Zambia are sneered at by petty patriots who use bureaucratic chicanery to protect their jobs, their status, their self-perceived superiority. Already Angola suffers from a chronic brain drain as qualified Angolan teachers, nurses, and administrators leave to earn more reliable salaries in Johannesburg, Lausanne, Baltimore, or Lisbon. White foreigners in white Land Rovers can temporarily help to bridge the gap in health provision and initiate the necessary vaccination and inoculation campaigns that will protect one cohort of infants. In 2003 seven million children were vaccinated in an effort to reduce Angola's horrendous infant mortality rate of 25 percent. Suitable long-term health plans need to be adopted by government.

The bombshell that might hit Angola now that peace has facilitated the free movement of people is a potential epidemic of HIV infection. No figures on current infection levels are reliable, though the Luanda maternity hospital did report an 8 percent incidence in 2001. The difficult balancing act will be to make people aware of the risks, including the risks brought by long-distance truckers now coming across the borders from highly infected areas in Namibia and Zambia, while avoiding starting a witch hunt that will target returnees from asylum as potential carriers of AIDS. Witch hunting has suddenly become not only a metaphor in Angola, but also a widely present practice. As people try to understand their malaise, their poverty, their ill health one year after the guns fell silent, they look to witchcraft as the evil force that blights their lives. The risks of AIDS are carried not only by "witches" and by returnees from countries where labor migration has fostered focal points of sexually transmitted infection, but also by men and women coming out of armies where unprotected sexual activity was rife. It is among the demobilized and among the cohorts of juveniles who never quite reached the age of conscription that HIV-awareness education needs to be most intense. Luanda's prime-time television showed a demure young lady stopping men on the street and asking them if they knew how to roll on a condom. Replies varied from Blimpish outrage at the very thought to open willingness to discuss the issue on camera. In the villages street theater takes the place of television and demonstrators get through a considerable supply of wooden penises during their performances before issuing free demonstration supplies in crowded rustic discos.

Street theater is also used to raise awareness of land mines and other abandoned ordnance that litter the roadside verges of the Angolan battlefields. Whether the number of land mines the armies left behind is one million or ten million is not known, but in some areas the risks are very real. Highly professional and experienced Angolan staff are clearing the highways, making the delivery of heavy food cheap by truck rather than expensive by air. Opening up farmland closed by minefields in order to coerce starving farmers to become army camp followers will take longer. Where the risk of mines is low and soil fertility is adequate, peasant men as well as women are hard at work. A return to the best maize land will, however, be bedeviled by legal disputes over title. Displaced farmers, returning refugees, demobilized conscripts all fear that any rich, well-watered tracts may fall into the hands of the country's ambitious generals with their cohorts of slick city lawyers and their blueprints for a return to colonial-style plantations.

In Angola the layers of government—municipal, provincial, and central—are not yet noted as purveyors of well-being. The country languishes alongside Uzbekistan at the bottom of the Human Development Index for oil-producing countries. The situation in the churches is somewhat more promising than in government. The Catholic Church runs its semifree radio station, but has not risked broadcasting any whispers of "liberation theology" and some radical priests with egalitarian sympathies—notably those from the Basque provinces of Spain—have been compelled to take home leave. In the last phase of the war one archbishop did win the Sakharov Prize for speaking out in favor of peace, liberty, and human rights. Other churchmen, however, aspire to join the generals in the ranks of the establishment and enroll their dependents and supporters into the private, very expensive Catholic university. The Methodist Church, historically the spiritual home of a radical, at one time even Marxist, segment of the city's elite, continues to flourish, and pew space was at a premium on Mother's Day when the venerable old bishop, who survived both the colonial oppression and the Marxist austerity, was in attendance alongside his young successor. Empowering the poor has been the agenda some of the churches have proposed. The more dynamic churches are Pentecostal, and it is to them that people have flocked during the years of insecurity. Congregations have mushroomed in ethnically mixed communities that have no traditional institutions of conflict resolution and where the church replaces kinship as the focus for a reconstructed society. Evangelical churches also flourish in the provinces, and Britain's parliamentary visitors were welcomed in the tradition of the Plymouth Brethren by a local pastor in one of the remotest villages in all Angola. He spoke no Portuguese but gently recounted in Lovale how his community was beginning to come back from the forests and rethatch its clay-built houses, harvest its surviving groves of cooking bananas, and rebuild its cultivation mounds of rich Zambezi alluvium. On such quiet firmness is the future of Angola based. Problems there may be, failings there may be too, but the spirit of hope lives on.

Notes

Chapter 1

1. For details of the creation of the Atlantic colonial system see David Birmingham, *Trade and Empire in the Atlantic, 1400–1600* (London: Routledge, 2000).

Chapter 2

1. José Mendes Ribeiro Norton de Matos, *Memórias e trabalhos da minha vida,* 4 vols. (Lisbon: Editora Marítimo-Colonial, 1944–45).
2. José Capela, *O vinho para o preto: notas e textos sobre a exportação do vinho para África* (Oporto: Afrontamento, 1973).
3. Charles von Onselen, *Studies in the Social and Economic History of the Witwatersrand,* 2 vols. (London: Longman, 1982). For a wider illumination of the role of alcohol in southern African society see Jonathan Crush and Charles Ambler, eds., *Liquor and Labor in Southern Africa* (Athens: Ohio University Press, 1992).
4. William A. Cadbury, *Labour in Portuguese West Africa* (London: G. Routledge, 1909).
5. An English edition of General Delgado's memoirs is available: Humberto da Silva Delgado, *The Memoirs of General Delgado* (London: Cassell, 1964); as well as a revised Portuguese edition: *Memórias de Humberto Delgado,* ed. Iva Delgado and Antonio de Figueiredo (Lisbon: Dom Quixote, 1991).

Chapter 3

1. David Birmingham, "Merchants and Missionaries in Angola," *Lusotopie* (1998): 345–55.

2. The latest and perhaps most lively of Beatrix Heintze's studies is *Pioneiros Africanos: caravanas de carregadores na África Centro-Ocidental entre 1850 e 1890* (Lisbon: Caminho, 2004).

3. David Livingstone, *Missionary Travels and Researches in South Africa* (London: J. Murray, 1857). For a gloss on Livingstone's visit to Angola see David Birmingham, *Portugal and Africa* (Athens: Ohio University Press, 2004).

4. Mary Kingsley, *West African Studies* (London: Macmillan, 1899).

5. The family biography of Héli Chatelain was written by his sister: Alida Chatelain and Amy Roch, *Héli Chatelain, l'ami de l'Angola, 1859–1908, fondateur de la Mission philafricaine d'après sa correspondence* (Lausanne: Mission Philafricaine, 1918). She makes extensive but selective use of his letter books. By very good fortune these letter books and other papers have survived in the archives of the Alliance Missionnaire Evangélique held by the Schweizer Allianz Mission in Winterthur. I am exceedingly grateful to the mission, and particularly to Albert Zimmerli, for the welcome hospitality that they have afforded me when working in Switzerland. Chapter 4 of the present book makes use of these papers to explore the second half of Chatelain's career and may, I hope, form the basis for a wider study of his life and times both as a member of the Luanda "Methodist" mission and as the founder of the Swiss mission at Kalukembe.

6. António Francisco Ferreira da Silva Porto, *Viagens e apontamentos de um Portuense em África*, ed. Maria Emília Madeira Santos (Coimbra: Coimbra University, 1986) is the first—and so far only—edited volume of Silva Porto's extensive archive. Frederick Stanley Arnot, *Missionary Travels in Central Africa* (London: Alfred Holness, 1914).

Chapter 4

1. In *A África e a instalacao do sistema colonial*, ed. Maria Emília Madeira Santos, 418–29 (Lisbon: IICT, 2000).

2. For a recent study of the Basel mission see Sonia Abun-Nasr, *Afrikaner und Missionar: Die Lebensgeschichte von David Asante* (Basel: Schlettwein, 2003).

3. Henry W. Nevinson, *A Modern Slavery* (London: Harper, 1906; reprint, Essex: Background Books, 1963). Nevinson's essays were first published in *Harper's* magazine in 1906.

Chapter 5

1. For further details and sources on Belgium and Portugal see David Birmingham, Muriel Chamberlain, and Chantal Metzger, *L'Europe et l'Afrique de 1914 à 1970* (Paris: SEDES, 1994), and also volume 2 of David Birmingham and Phyllis M. Martin, *History of Central Africa* (London: Longman, 1983).

2. See 'The Coffee Barons of Cazengo," in Birmingham, *Portugal and Africa.*

Chapter 6

1. Christine Messiant, *L'Angola colonial: histoire et société* (Basel: Schlettwein, forthcoming).

2. Basil Davidson, *The African Awakening* (London: Cape, 1955).

Chapter 7

1. Marcelo Bittencourt, *"Estamos juntos": o MPLA e a luta anticolonial* (Luanda: Angolan National Archives, forthcoming).

2. Drumond Jaime and Helder Barber, eds., *Angola: depoimentos para a história recente,* vol. 1 (Lisbon: Drumond Jaime and Helder Barber, 1999).

Chapter 8

1. David Birmingham, *Frontline Nationalism in Angola and Mozambique* (Trenton, NJ: Africa World Press; London: James Currey, 1992).

2. Fred Bridgland, *Jonas Savimbi: A Key to Africa* (Edinburgh: Mainstream, 1986).

Chapter 9

1. David Birmingham, "O carnaval em Luanda," *Análise Social* 26 (1991): 417–29; Birmingham, "Carnival at Luanda," *Journal of African History* 29, no. 1 (1988): 93–103.

2. Ralph Delgado, *História de Angola,* 4 vols. (Lobito: Ralph Delgado, 1948–53). Two promised later volumes appear not to have been completed, but Delgado did also write books on Benguela and its hinterland,

both as history and in the form of a novel, *O Amor a 12 graus de latitude sul* (Oporto: Emprêsa Industrial Gráfica, 1935).

3. Rui Duarte de Carvalho, "Ana Manda—les enfants du filet: identité collective, créativité sociale et production de la différence culturelle: un cas Muxiluanda" (PhD diss., L'École des Hautes Etudes en Sciences Sociales, Paris, 1986).

4. Terence Ranger, *Dance and Society in Eastern Africa, 1890–1970: The Beni Ngoma* (Berkeley: University of California Press; London: Heinemann, 1975).

Chapter 10

1. Patrick Chabal, ed., *A History of Postcolonial Lusophone Africa* (Bloomington: Indiana University Press; London: Christopher Hurst, 2002).

2. Christine Messiant, "The Eduardo dos Santos Foundation: Or, how Angola's Regime is Taking over Civil Society," *African Affairs* 100 (2001): 287–309.

3. Tony Hodges, *Angola: From Afro-Stalinism to Petro-Diamond Capitalism* (Bloomington: Indiana University Press; Oxford: James Currey, 2001).

Chapter 11

1. All-Party Parliamentary Group for Angola, *Impressions and Recommendations on a Visit to Angola, 3–10 May 2003* (London: Royal Institute for International Affairs, 2003).

2. Transparency International Corruption Perceptions Index 2003, http://www.transparency.org/cpi/2003/cpi2003.en.html. In the 2004 index Angola was at number 133.

Further Reading

Birmingham, David. *A Concise History of Portugal*. 2nd ed. Cambridge: Cambridge University Press, 2003. Translated into Portuguese by Ana Mafalda Tello as *História de Portugal: uma perspectiva mundial* (Lisbon: Terramar, 1998).

———. *The Decolonization of Africa*. Athens: Ohio University Press; London: Routledge, 1995.

———. *Portugal and Africa*. Athens: Ohio University Press, 2004. Translated into Portuguese by Arlindo Barbeitos as *Portugal e África* (Lisbon: Vega, 2003).

———. *Trade and Conflict in Angola: The Mbundu and Their Neighbours under the Influence of the Portuguese, 1483–1790*. Oxford: Clarendon Press, 1966. Translated into Portuguese by João B. Borges as *Alianças e conflitos: os primórdios da ocupação estrangeira em Angola, 1483–1790* (Luanda: Arquivo Histórico de Angola, 2004).

———. *Trade and Empire in the Atlantic, 1400–1600*. London: Routledge, 2000.

Birmingham, David, and Phyllis M. Martin. *History of Central Africa*. 2 vols. London: Longman, 1983.

———. *History of Central Africa: The Contemporary Years; Since 1960*. London: Longman, 1998.

Bittencourt, Marcelo. *"Estamos juntos": o MPLA e a luta anticolonial*. Luanda: Angolan National Archives, forthcoming

Clarence-Smith, William Gervase. *Slaves, Peasants and Capitalists in Southern Angola, 1840–1926*. Cambridge: Cambridge University Press, 1979.

———. *The Third Portuguese Empire, 1825–1975: A Study in Economic Imperialism*. Manchester: Manchester University Press, 1985.

Coppé, Margrit, and Fergus Power, eds. *Stories for Trees: Stories and Images of Angola*. Luanda: Development Workshop, 2002.

Davidson, Basil. *The African Awakening*. London: Cape, 1955.

——. *The Black Man's Burden: Africa and the Curse of the Nation-State.* New York: Times Books, 1992.

——. *Black Mother: The Years of the African Slave Trade.* Boston: Little, Brown, 1961.

——. *In the Eye of the Storm: Angola's People.* Garden City, NY: Doubleday, 1972.

Dias, Jill. "Angola." In *Nova história da expansão Portuguesa,* vol. 10, 319–556. Lisbon: Estampa, 1998.

Ferreira, Manuel Ennes. *A indústria em tempo de guerra: Angola 1975–91.* Lisbon: Cosmos, 1999.

Freudenthal, Aïda. "Angola." In *Nova história da expansão Portuguesa,* vol. 11, 259–417. Lisbon: Estampa, 2001.

——. *Arimos e fazendas: a transição agrária em Angola.* Luanda: Caxinde, 2005.

Heintze, Beatrix. *Pioneiros Africanos: Caravanas de carregadores na África Centro-Ocidental entre 1850 e 1890.* Lisbon: Caminho, 2004.

Jaime, Drumond, and Helder Barber, eds. *Angola: depoimentos para a história recente.* Vol. 1. Lisbon: Drumond Jaime and Helder Barber, 1999.

Kapuscinski, Ryszard. *Another Day of Life.* Translated by William R. Brand and Katarzyna Mroczkowska-Brand. London: Pan, 1987.

Lara, Lúcio. *Um amplo movimento: itinerário do MPLA através de documentos e anotações de Lúcio Lara.* Vol. 1. Luanda: Ruth and Lúcio Lara, 1997.

Mabeko-Tali, Jean-Michel. *Barbares et citoyens: l'identité nationale à l'épreuve des transitions africaines: Congo-Brazzaville, Angola.* Paris: Harmattan, 2005.

——. *Dissidências e poder de estado: o MPLA perante si próprio, 1962–1977.* 2 vols. Translated from French to Portuguese by Manuel Ruas. Luanda: Editorial Nzila, 2001.

Maier, Karl. *Angola: Promises and Lies.* London: Serif, 1996.

Marcum, John A. *The Angolan Revolution.* 2 vols. Cambridge, MA: MIT Press, 1969–1978.

Marques, João Pedro. *The Sounds of Silence: Nineteenth-Century Portugal and the Abolition of the Slave Trade.* Translated by Richard Wall. Oxford: Berghahn, 2005.

Martin, Phyllis M. *Leisure and Society in Colonial Brazzaville.* Cambridge: Cambridge University Press, 1995.

Mendes, Pedro Rosa. *Baía dos tigres.* Lisbon: Dom Quixote, 1999. Translated by Clifford Landers as *Bay of Tigers: An African Odyssey.* Orlando: Harcourt, 2003.

Messiant, Christine. *L'Angola colonial: histoire et société*. Basel: Schlettwein, forthcoming.

———. "Luanda (1945–1961): colonisés, société coloniale et engagement nationaliste." In *Bourgs et villes en Afrique lusophone*, edited by Michel Cahen, 125–200. Paris: Harmattan, 1989.

———. "Em Angola, até o passado é imprevisível." In *Construindo o passado angolano: as fontes e a sua interpretação*, 803–59. Lisbon: Comissão Nacional para as Comemorações dos Descobrimentos Portugueses, 2000.

Miller, Joseph C. *Way of Death: Merchant Capitalism and the Angolan Slave Trade, 1730–1830*. Madison: University of Wisconsin Press, 1988.

Nascimento, Augusto. *Desterro e contrato: Moçambicanos a caminho de S. Tomé e Príncipe, 1940–1960*. Maputo: Arquivo Histórico de Moçambique, 2002.

Nevinson, Henry W. *A Modern Slavery*. London: Harper, 1906. Reprint, Essex: Background Books, 1963.

Newitt, M. D. D. *A History of Mozambique*. London: Hurst, 1995.

———. *Portuguese Settlement on the Zambesi: Exploration, Land Tenure and Colonial Rule in East Africa*. Harlow: Longman, 1973.

Péclard, Didier. "Etat colonial, missions chrétiennes et nationalisme en Angola, 1920–1975: aux racines sociales de l'UNITA." PhD diss, IEP Paris, 2005.

Pepetela (Artur Carlos Maurício Pestana). *Mayombe*. Translated by Michael Wolfers. London: Heinemann, 1983.

———. *The Return of the Water Spirit*. Translated by Luís R. Mitras. Oxford: Heinemann, 2002.

———. *Yaka*. Translated by Marga Holness. Oxford: Heinemann, 1996.

Vos, Jelmer. "The Kingdom of Kongo and Its Borderlands." PhD diss., London University, 2005.

Walker, John Frederick. *A Certain Curve of Horn: The Hundred-Year Quest for the Giant Sable Antelope of Angola*. New York: Atlantic Monthly Press, 2002.

The novels of Artur Pestana, who writes under the pen name Pepetela, are some of the most valuable works in the canon of Angolan literature and illuminate the country's historical experience from the seventeenth to the twenty-first centuries as no other source can. Only *Mayombe* (1983), *Yaka* (1996), and *Desejo de Kianda* (The Return of the Water Spirit) (2002) are available in English. The other half-dozen works urgently deserve to be made available to a wider audience, notably the legend of the old tortoise, which graphically displays the wartime experiences of rural Angolans, and the detective adventures of Jaime Bunda, which portray the aspirations and fears of city dwellers.

The essays of Christine Messiant, predominantly in French but a few in English and Portuguese, are the most important collection of academic works on the contemporary history of Angola, beginning with her essay on Luanda (1989) and culminating in her perceptively humorous Portuguese lecture describing how in Angola even the past is unpredictable (2000). The book version of Messiant's doctoral thesis is forthcoming from Schlettwein in Basel and an anthology of her writings is in preparation at Karthala in Paris.

Two of the most important historical studies of Angola to have appeared in Portuguese are in the *Nova história da expansão Portuguesa*. Jill Dias has written the most comprehensive survey so far attempted of nineteenth-century Angola's history. She has drawn on her thirty years of archival research and her long-running editorship of the *Revista Internacional de Estudos Africanos*. Aïda Freudenthal carries the story forward, also at near book length, with perceptive insights carried forward to 1930. More recently she has published *Arimos e fazendas: a transição agrária em Angola* (2005). João Pedro Marques (2005) has written an important innovative study of the changing imperial attitudes of Portugal in the nineteenth century. The irony of Marques's title, *The Sounds of Silence*, when referring to Portugal and the abolition of the slave trade, is highlighted by the work of Augusto Nascimento (2002), which documents the continuing transoceanic trade in convicts and exiles in the 1950s. A study of more recent history, focusing on Angola with a good economic emphasis, is by Manuel Ennes Ferreira (1999).

In Germany, Beatrix Heintze's extensive pioneering studies, in Portuguese as well as in German, cover many aspects of Angola's experience from the seventeenth century onward. Her latest book, *Pioneiros Africanos*, contains brilliant vignettes of daily life on the colonial frontier.

In Britain, two scholars have made great contributions to the understanding of Portuguese imperial activities in Africa. Gervase Clarence-Smith followed up his *Slaves, Peasants and Capitalists in Southern Angola, 1840–1926* (1979) with a pathbreaking survey, *The Third Portuguese Empire 1825–1975* (1985). Malyn Newitt similarly followed up his focused study of Zambezi colonization, *Portuguese Settlement on the Zambesi* (1973), with a comprehensively documented survey, *A History of Mozambique* (1995). The latest London University doctorate on Angola is by Jelmer Vos, *The Kingdom of Kongo and its Borderlands 1885–1913* (2005).

My own work on Angola includes a companion volume to the present one, *Portugal and Africa* (2004), with fifteen essays on topics from Iron Age commercial history to the postcolonial urban rebellion of 1977. Aspects of the comparisons between Angola and its neighbors will be found in the three volumes of the Longman *History of Central Africa* (1983, 1998), which I edited with Phyllis M. Martin, a historian who wrote the classic study *Leisure and Society in Colonial Brazzaville* (1995). *Alianças e conflitos* (2004) is the Portuguese edition of my *Trade and Conflict in Angola* (1966). For the imperial context of empire see *A Concise History of Portugal* (2nd ed., 2003), and for the context of decolonization see *The Decolonization of Africa* (1995). See also my companion volume to *Decolonization*, a work dealing with the origins of the Atlantic empires, *Trade and Empire in the Atlantic, 1400–1600* (2000).

Scholars in the United States have produced extensive and excellent work on Angola. One of the most fundamental books ever written on the country is Joseph C. Miller's *Way of Death* (1988). For the twentieth century the classic two-volume study is John A. Marcum's *Angolan Revolution* (1969–1978). More recently, in a rather different vein, John Frederick Walker came to understand Angola very well when conducting his study of ecological survival in a war zone, a story written up in *A Certain Curve of Horn* (2002).

Many travelers have recorded their impressions of Angola over many centuries. Henry W. Nevinson's *Modern Slavery* (1906) is a travel diary whose observations on the nature of early twentieth-century slavery were published in *Harper's* magazine and confirmed at the time by William A. Cadbury and Héli Chatelain. Basil Davidson's *African Awakening* (1955) describes a journey into Angola and the Congo by a scholar who went on to observe the region closely for fifty years. Other relevant works by Davidson include *Black Mother* (1961), *In the Eye of the Storm* (1972), and *The Black Man's Burden* (1992), which is perhaps the most ambitious attempt yet to survey the imperial legacy in Africa. A third traveler whose eye leaves a lasting legacy is Ryszard Kapuscinski (*Another Day of Life*, 1987) a Polish journalist who experienced the birth pangs of the Angolan republic. Another outstanding journalist came from America to experience the daily life of war-torn Angola and record his sympathetic insights: Karl Maier, *Angola: Promises and Lies* (1996). A fifth distinguished observer, who saw more of Angola than most and wrote with unrivaled perception, is Pedro Rosa Mendes (*Baía dos tigres*, 1999).

Inside Angola, new works of great insight are beginning to be published. *Stories for Trees* (2002), edited by Margrit Coppé and Fergus Power, contains not only charming vignettes of daily life under the shadow of war but also a fine photographic record of the late twentieth century. A much heavier documentary work, *Angola: depoimentos para a história recente*, the first volume of which was edited by Drumond Jaime and Helder Barber in 1999, contains transcripts of interviews with many of Angola's leading citizens. One such leading citizen and intellectual was Lúcio Lara, and although he never wrote his own autobiography, his friends assembled a collection of his writings: *Um amplo movimento* (1997). A two-volume history of the party to which Lara belonged has been published by Jean-Michel Mabeko-Tali, *Dissidências e poder de estado*. A French study by Mabeko-Tali, *Barbares et citoyens* (2005), compares the search for national identity in Angola and in its northern neighbor, Congo-Brazzaville. A Brazilian dissertation by Marcelo Bittencourt, "Estamos juntos" (to be published by the Angolan National Archives), will provide new insights into the war of decolonization, which stretched Angola's peoples to the limit from 1961 to 1974.

A little fresh archival material, and some new travel experiences, have enlivened the essays in this book. The archives of the Swiss mission in Angola, safely preserved over the years in the mission headquarters at Winterthur, were a fund of inspiration. In Luanda the national archive contains unbelievable quantities of documentation sent to the capital from the provinces at various points in time. The collection that I most recently consulted concerns the highland district of Caconda, where the Swiss polymath, preacher, linguist, and wagon merchant Héli Chatelain built his Christian village. His insights were what inspired me to put this collection of essays together.

Index

Printed and bound by CPI Group (UK) Ltd, Croydon, CR0 4YY

09/06/2025